Like a Bundle of Reeds

Why Unity
and
Mutual Guarantee
are
Today's Call of the Hour

LAITMAN
KABBALAH
PUBLISHERS

T0163064

Michael Laitman, PhD

Like a Bundle of Reeds

Why unity and mutual guarantee
are today's call of the hour

Copyright © 2013 by Michael Laitman

All rights reserved
Published by Laitman Kabbalah Publishers
www.bundleofreeds.com   contact@bundleofreeds.com
1057 Steeles Avenue West, Suite 532, Toronto,
ON, M2R 3X1, Canada

2009 85th Street #51, Brooklyn, New York, 11214, USA

Printed in Canada

ISBN: 978-1-897448-82-3
Library of Congress Control Number: 2013934876

Research: Norma Livne, Masha Shayovich, Sarin David, David
Melnitchuk, Christiane Reinstrom, Kristian Dawson,
Dr. David Martino, Ciro Grossi
Proof Reading: Debbie Sirt, Veronica Edwards, Julian Edwards
Associate Editors: Oded Spiegler, Jesse Bogner, Mary Miesem
Copy Editor: Claire Gerus
Layout: Baruch Khovov
Cover: Rony Perry, Inna Smirnova
Executive Editor: Chaim Ratz
Printing and Post Production: Uri Laitman

FIRST EDITION: JANUARY 2014
First Printing

CONTENTS

The Specter and the Spirit

How I came to write this book

I was born in August, 1946 in the city of Vitebsk, Belarus. It was the second summer after the end of World War Two, and life was sluggish, slowly hobbling back toward the affable monotony of normalcy. Being the firstborn child of a dentist father and a gynecologist mother, I had a rather carefree childhood, conveniently growing up in a suburban neighborhood, untroubled by the material concerns that preoccupied most of my childhood friends.

And yet, a shadow followed me throughout my childhood and even through my teens. It was the specter of the Holocaust, that phantom many chose never to mention, though it was always there. Names of family members or of friends who perished were mentioned in a somber tone, giving them an uncanny presence, as though they were still with us, although I knew they weren't.

And odder still was the revulsion of my Russian peers toward Jews. Children I grew up with hated Jews simply because they were Jews. They knew what had happened to their Jewish neighbors just over a year ago, but they were as sardonic and unsympathetic as before the war, so I was told by my elders. This, I could not understand. Why were they so hateful? What unforgivable wrong had Jews ever done to them? And where did they learn those horror stories about the things that Jews might do to them?

As would be expected from the son of parents in the medical professions, I, too, took up a medical profession as my career "of choice." I studied medical bio-cybernetics, a science that explores the systems of the human body, and I became a scientist, a researcher at the St. Petersburg Blood Research Institute. And while fantasizing myself beaming with pride on the pulpit in Stockholm, Sweden, the winner of a Nobel Prize, a deeper passion I have been harboring has been edging toward the surface of my consciousness.

"I want to understand *the system*," I began to think, "to know how *everything works*." But most of all, I began to ponder *why* everything was the way it was.

As a scientist at heart, I began to search for scientific answers that could explain *everything*, not just how to calculate the mass of an object or the acceleration of its fall, but what caused that object to exist *in the first place*.

And since I could not find an answer in science, I decided to move on. After being a *refusenik* (Soviet Jews who were denied permission to emigrate abroad) for two years, I finally got my permit and left for Israel in 1974.

In Israel, I kept searching for the meaning and the reason behind everything. Two years after I arrived in Israel,

I began to study Kabbalah. But it was not until February, 1979 that I found my teacher, the Rabash, the firstborn son and successor of Rav Yehuda Leib HaLevi Ashlag, known as Baal HaSulam (Owner of the Ladder) for his *Sulam* (Ladder) commentary on *The Book of Zohar*.

Finally, my prayers were answered! Each day, each hour, new revelations dawned on me. The pieces of the puzzle of reality fell into place one at a time, and a coherent picture of the world began to form before me, as though the mist itself was taking shape before my awestruck eyes.

My life had been transformed, and I immersed myself in my studies and in assisting the Rabash in any way I could. I was fortunate enough to be able to support my family with just a few hours of work each day, and I dedicated the rest of my time to absorbing the wisdom as much and as deeply as I could.

To me, I was living a dream reality. I had a wonderful family, I lived in a country where I really felt free; I made a good living with ease, and I had found the answers to my lifelong questions.

One of those persistent questions was the one about the hatred of the Jews. In Kabbalah, I discovered why it happens, why it is persisting, and most important, what must be done to heal it. Indeed, anti-Semitism is a sore in the heart of humanity, an echo of an unhealed pain that the world has been carrying for almost 4,000 years, since Abraham, our Patriarch, left Babylon.

Kabbalah has taught me that Abraham had proposed to his people to unite and be once more of "one language and of one speech" (Genesis 11:1), and that King Nimrod, Babylon's ruler at the time, had prevented Abraham from circulating his idea. Gradually, I came to see that what the world now needs is that same unity, that camaraderie and mutual guarantee that Abraham had developed with his group and progeny, and that King Nimrod had stopped him from endowing to his Babylonian brothers and sisters.

One morning lesson, my teacher, the Rabash, taught me Baal HaSulam's "Introduction to the Book of Zohar." At the end of it, Baal HaSulam wrote that unless the Jews endowed the world with the knowledge and the guidance toward unity, the nations of the world would loathe the Jews, humiliate them, drive them out from the land of Israel, and torment them wherever they may be. I had read that unfathomable essay before, but that morning it had a deeper impact on me. I felt another stage in my development emerging from within.

Later that day, we went to Kfar Saba, a small town near Tel Aviv, to a Kolel (Jewish seminary) named after my esteemed mentor. In the basement, the Rabash showed me a medium-size cardboard box filled to the brim with handwritten pieces of paper. He asked if I could take it to the car and bring it back to his house.

I put the box in the trunk, and on the way back I asked him what those papers were in the box. Unceremoniously, he muttered, "Some old manuscripts of Baal HaSulam." I looked at him, but he looked straight at the road ahead and kept silent all the way back.

That night, the lights were on in Baruch Ashlag's kitchen all night long. I stayed there and meticulously read through every piece of paper until I found one that would let me search no more. It was the piece of the puzzle I was looking for without even knowing it. It was the capstone, the first step in the march I was to take henceforth.

The paper I had found, which is now part of Baal HaSulam's "The Writings of the Last Generation," told a tale of agony and thirst, love and friendship, deliverance and commitment. Here are the words that I found: "There is an allegory about friends who were lost in the desert, hungry and thirsty. One of them had found a settlement filled abundantly with every delight. He remembered his poor brothers, but he had already drawn far off from them and did not know their place. ...He began to shout out loud and blow the horn; perhaps his poor, hungry friends would hear his voice, approach and come to that abundant settlement filled with every delight.

"So is the matter before us: we have been lost in the terrible desert along with all of humanity, and now we have found a great, abundant treasure, namely the books of Kabbalah. They fulfill our yearning souls and fill us abundantly with lushness and agreement.

"We are satiated and there is more, but the memory of our friends left hopelessly in the terrible desert remains deep within our hearts. The distance is great, and words cannot bridge between us. For this reason, we have set up this horn to blow loudly so that our brothers may hear and draw near and be as happy as we.

"Know, our brothers, our flesh, that the essence of the wisdom of Kabbalah consists of the knowledge of how the world came down from its elevated, heavenly place, to our ignoble state. ...It is therefore very easy to find in the wisdom of Kabbalah all the future corrections destined to come from the perfect worlds that preceded us. Through it we will know how to correct our ways henceforth.

"...Imagine, for example, that some historic book were to be found today, which depicts the last generations ten thousand years from now, describing the comportment of both individuals and society. Our leaders would seek out every counsel to arrange life here accordingly, and we would come to 'no outcry in our broad places.' Corruption and the terrible suffering would cease, and everything would come peacefully to its place.

"Now, distinguished readers, this book lies here before you in a closet. It states explicitly the entire wisdom of statesmanship and the conducts of private and public life that will exist at the end of days. It is the books of Kabbalah, where the corrected worlds are set. ...Open these books and you will find all the good comportments that will appear at the end of days, and you will find within them the good lessons by which to arrange mundane matters today as well.

"...I can no longer restrain myself. I have resolved to disclose the conducts of correction of our definite future that I have found by observation and by reading in these books. I have decided to go out to the people of the world with this horn, and I believe and estimate that it shall suffice to gather all those deserving to begin to study and delve in the books. Thus they will sentence themselves and the entire world to a scale of merit."[1]

About a year after finding these papers, I published my first three books with my teacher's guidance and support. I have been publishing books ever since, and I have circulated Kabbalah by numerous other means, as well.

Today's reality is very harsh, and people often have no patience or desire to delve into books, as Baal HaSulam imagined. But the essence of the wisdom, the love, and the unity that are the foundations of reality, and which Kabbalah instills in its practitioners, remain as true as they have always been.

Moreover, since around the turn of the century, anti-Semitism has been on the rise once more, this time the world over. The specter of the hatred of the Jews has taken root worldwide. Spreading stealthily and venomously, it is threatening to infest entire nations with Judeophobia, and to repeat the horrors of the past.

But now we know the cure. Whenever Jews unite, the serpent hides its head. The spirit of camaraderie and mutual responsibility has always been our "weapon," our shield against adversity. Now we should muster that spirit, cloak ourselves with it, and let its healing warmth surround us. And once we have done so, we must share that spirit with the rest of the world, as this is our vocation—the essence of our being "a light for the nations."

And so, because we all need answers to our deepest questions, because deep inside all Jews want to know the cure for anti-Semitism, and because it is the legacy of my teacher and my teacher's great teacher and father, I have decided to detail what I have learned from them. They taught me what it means to be a Jew, what it means to be committed, and what it means to share. But most of all, they taught me what it means to love like the Creator.

INTRODUCTION

"If a person takes a bundle of reeds, he cannot break them all at once. But taken one at a time, even an infant will break them. Just so, Israel will not be redeemed until they are all one bundle."

(Midrash *Tanhuma*, *Nitzavim*, Chapter 1)

Throughout the history of the Jewish people, unity and mutual guarantee (otherwise known as mutual responsibility) have been the emblems of our nation. Countless sages and spiritual leaders have written about the significance of these two trademarks, hailing them as the heart and soul of our nation, and declaring that salvation and redemption can arrive only when there is unity in Israel.

In fact, the concept of unity has been so preeminent, it has exceeded that of devotion to the Creator and the observance of commandments. A considerable number of Jewish spiritual leaders and sacred texts throughout the generations stress the importance of unity above all else. *Masechet Derech Eretz Zuta*, written at approximately the same time as the Talmud, is one of numerous statements in that spirit: "Even when Israel worship idols and there is peace among them, the Lord says, 'I have no wish to harm them.' ...But if they are disputed, what is it that is said about them? 'Their heart is divided; now they will bear their guilt.'"[2]

After the ruin of the Second Temple, the preeminence of unity and brotherly love peaked. The Babylonian Talmud, among many other sources, teaches us that the reason why the Second Temple was ruined was unfounded hatred and divisiveness within Israel. The sources even declare that unfounded hatred is so harmful, it equals the impact of the three great evils that caused the ruin of the First Temple, put together: idolatry, incest, and bloodshed. *Masechet Yoma* teaches us that lesson very clearly: "The Second Temple ... why was it ruined? It was because there was unfounded hatred in it, teaching you that unfounded hatred is equal to all three transgressions—idolatry, incest, and bloodshed—combined."[3]

Evidently, unity, brotherhood, and mutual guarantee are not only in the DNA of our nation, they are the substance of the lifeline that has spared us afflictions when we had them, and allowed for afflictions to unfold when we did not. In these trying times of distended self-entitlement and narcissism, we need unity more than ever, yet it seems more inaccessible than at any time in history.

Some thirty-four centuries ago, at the foot of Mount Sinai, we stood as one man with one heart, and by so doing we became a nation. Since then, unity has sustained us through rain and shine, as renowned preacher and writer, Rabbi Kalonymus Kalman Halevi Epstein, describes in his acclaimed composition, *Maor va Shemesh* (*Light and Sun*): "Although the generation of Ahab were idol worshippers, they engaged in war and won because there was unity among them. It is even more so when there is unity in Israel and they engage in Torah for Her sake ... By that, they subdue all who are against them, and everything they say with their mouths, the Lord grants their wishes."[4]

Following Moses, we came to Canaan, conquered it, made it The Land of Israel, and then were exiled once again, this time to Babel. And once Mordechai united us in Babel, we returned, though barely two of the original twelve tribes, and established the Second Temple. As long as we kept our unity, we also kept our sovereignty and the Temple. But once we relinquished brotherly love, we were overwhelmed by the enemy and were exiled for centuries to come.

Yet, division and unfounded hatred, which caused the ruin of the Second Temple and the exile of the nation from its land, did not arrest our development while in exile. Through much of the last two or so millennia, we kept to ourselves, maintaining relative separation from the cultural life of the nations in which we resided.

But roughly since the time of the Enlightenment, we have gradually adopted a culture that hails personal distinction and individual achievement, and condones exploitation of the weak and needy. In the last several decades, we have so excelled at the culture of self-interest and self-entitlement that as a society, we have become the complete opposite of the caring and humane community we nurtured at the onset of our nation.

In today's world, the reigning tone and atmosphere are of self-entitlement and egotism to the point of narcissism. In their insightful book, *The Narcissism Epidemic: Living in the Age of Entitlement*, psychologists Jean M. Twenge and Keith

Campbell describe what they refer to as "The relentless rise of narcissism in our culture,"[5] and the problems it causes. They explain that "The United States is currently suffering from an epidemic of narcissism. ...narcissistic personality traits rose just as fast as obesity."

Worse yet, they continue, "The rise in narcissism is accelerating, with scores rising faster in the 2000s than in previous decades. By 2006, one out of four college students agreed with the majority of the items on a standard measure of narcissistic traits."[6]

And the majority of us Jews, progenitors of the tenet, "Love your neighbor as yourself," not only sit by and watch as egotism celebrates, but also join the party, many of us even leading the pack, taking spoils wherever we can. We have embraced the maxim, "When in Rome, do as the Romans do," with spectacular enthusiasm, and by so doing, many Jewish names have become synonymous with wealth and power. There is no doubt that we do not pursue wealth and power to present our heritage as superior to those of others. However, when Jews gain notoriety for the above two distinctions, they are noted not only for their gains, but also for their heritage.

As unfair as it may seem, Jews and the Jewish state are not viewed in the same manner as are other countries and nations. They are treated as special, both positively and negatively.

But there is a good reason why this is so. When Abraham discovered the singular force that leads the world, the one we refer to as "the Creator," "God," *HaShem, HaVaYaH* (*Yod-Hey-Vav-Hey*, the "Lord"), he wished to tell the whole world about it. As a Babylonian of high social and spiritual status, the son of a maker of idols and statues, he was in a position to be heard. It was only when King Nimrod tried to kill him and later expelled him from Babylon that he went elsewhere, eventually arriving at Canaan.

Yet, Rav Moshe Ben Maimon (Maimonides) describes how all along the way he kept looking for soul mates with whom he could share his discovery: "He began to call out to the whole world, to alert them that there is one God to the whole world... He was calling out, wandering from town to town and from kingdom to kingdom, until he arrived in the land of Canaan... And since they [people in the places where he wandered] gathered around him and asked him about his words, he taught everyone...until he brought them back to the path of truth. Finally, thousands and tens of thousands assembled around him, and they are the people of 'the house of Abraham.' He planted this tenet in their hearts, composed books about it, and taught his son, Isaac. And Isaac sat, and taught, warned, and informed Jacob, and appointed him a teacher, to sit and teach... And Jacob the Patriarch taught all his sons, and separated Levi and appointed him the head, and had him sit and learn the way of God..."[7]

From Jacob onward, narrates the renowned composition, *The Kozari*, "Godliness is revealed in an assembly, and since then is the count by which we count the years of the ancestors, according to what was given to us in Moses' law [Torah], and we know what unfolded since Moses to this day."[8]

Thus, unity became a condition for attaining the perception of God, or the Creator—as Kabbalists often refer to Him (for reasons we will not detail here, as it is beyond the scope of this book). Without unity, attainment was simply impossible. Those who were able to unite became the people of Israel and attained the Creator, the singular force that creates, governs, and leads the whole of reality. Those who weren't able to do so remained without that perception, yet with a sense that the Israelites knew something that they did not, and had something that belonged to them, as well, but that they could not have.

This is the root of the hatred of Israel, which later became anti-Semitism. It is a feeling that the Jews have something that they aren't sharing with the world, but which they must.

Indeed, the Jews must share it with the world. Just as Abraham tried to share his discovery with all his fellow Babylonians, the Jews, his descendants, must do the same. This is the meaning of being "A light for the nations." This is the obligation to which the great Rav Kook, the first Chief Rabbi of Israel, referred in his eloquent, poetic style when he wrote, "The genuine movement of the Israeli soul at its grandest is expressed only by its sacred, eternal force, which flows within its spirit. It is that which has made it, is making it, and will make it still a nation that stands as a light unto nations, as redemption and salvation to the entire world for its own specific purpose, and for the global purposes, which are interlinked."[9]

This commitment is also that to which Rav Yehuda Leib Arie Altar referred with his words, "The children of Israel are guarantors in that they received the Torah in order to correct the whole world, the nations, too."[10]

And what exactly is it that we are obliged to pass on to the nations? It is unity, through which one discovers life's unique, singular creating force, the Lord, or God.

In the words of Rabbi Shmuel Bornstein, author of *Shem MiShmuel* [*A Name Out of Samuel*], "The aim of Creation was for all to be one association ... But because of the sin, the matter became so spoiled that even the best in those generations were unable to unite together to serve the Lord, but were a few, alone."[11]

For this reason, continues Rabbi Bornstein, only those who could unite did so, while the rest parted from them until they were able to join the unity. In his words, "The correction began with making a gathering and association of people to serve the Creator, beginning with Abraham the Patriarch and his descendents, so they would be a consolidated community for the work of God. His [the Creator's] idea in separating people was that first He caused separation in the human race, at the time of Babylon, and all the evildoers were dispersed. ...Subsequently began the gathering in order to serve the Creator, as Abraham the Patriarch went and called by the name of the Lord until a great community gathered toward him, who had been called 'the people of the house of Abraham.' The matter continued to grow until it became the assembly of the congregation of Israel ... and the end of correction will be in the future, when everyone becomes one association in order to do Your will wholeheartedly."[12]

Considering the current global circumstances, it seems urgent that everyone know about the concept of unity as a means of attaining the Creator. Once all of us know and accept that tenet, peace and brotherhood will naturally prevail.

In fact, according to renowned Kabbalist, Rav Yehuda Ashlag, known as Baal HaSulam [Owner of the Ladder] for his *Sulam* [Ladder] commentary on *The Book of*

Zohar, the need to know the Creator has been urgent for almost a century now. In "Peace in the World," an essay dating back to the early 1930s, Baal HaSulam explains that because we are all interdependent, we must apply the laws of mutual guarantee to the entire world. While the term, "globalization," was not as ubiquitous in treatises of his time, his words clearly illustrate his urgent need to make the world a single, solidified unit.

Here is Baal HaSulam's description of globalization and interdependence: "Do not be surprised if I mix together the well-being of a particular collective with the well-being of the whole world, because indeed, we have already come to such a degree that the whole world is considered one collective and one society. That is, because each person in the world draws one's life's marrow and livelihood from all the people in the world, one is coerced to serve and care for the well-being of the entire world.

"...Therefore, the possibility of making good, happy, and peaceful conducts in one country is inconceivable when it is not so in all the countries in the world, and vice versa. In our time, the countries are all linked in the satisfaction of their needs of life, as individuals were in their families in earlier times. Therefore, we can no longer speak or deal with just conducts that guarantee the well-being of one country or one nation, but only with the well-being of the whole world because the benefit or harm of each and every person in the world depends and is measured by the benefit of all the people in the world."[13]

However, for the world to achieve that unity, that mutual guarantee, it needs a role model, a group or collective that can implement unity, attain the Creator, and by personal example, pave the way for the rest of humankind. Because we Jews had already been at that point, and the world subconsciously feels it, it is our duty to rekindle that brotherly love among us, attain that singular force, and pass on both the method of unity and the attainment of the Creator to the rest of the world. This is the role of the Jews: to bring the light of the Creator to the world, to be a light to the nations.

In "The Love of God and the Love of Man," Baal HaSulam clearly describes that *modus operandi*: "The Israeli nation has been established as a transition. To the same extent that Israel themselves are purified by keeping the Torah [the law (of unity), which we said in the introduction was a precondition for attainment of the Creator], they pass on their power to the rest of the nations. And when the rest of the nations also sentence themselves to a scale of merit [unite and attain the Creator], the Messiah [the force that pulls us out of egoism] will be revealed."[14]

Rav Yehuda Altar similarly describes the role of Jews in regard to the rest of the nations: "It would seem that the children of Israel, the recipients of the Torah, are the borrowers and not the guarantors, except that the children of Israel became responsible for the correction of the entire world by the power of the Torah. This is why it was said to them, 'And you will be unto Me a kingdom of priests and a holy nation.' ...And it is to that that they replied, 'That which the Lord has said, we shall do'—correct the whole of Creation. ...In truth, everything depends on the children of Israel. As much as they correct themselves, all creations follow them. As the students follow the rav [teacher] who corrects himself ... similarly, the whole of Creation follows the children of Israel."[15]

CHAPTER 1

A Nation Is Born

The Birth of the People of Israel

Before we delve into the significance and position of the people of Israel in the world, we need to look into why the Israeli nation formed, and how that forming unfolded. Let us, for a moment, journey roughly six thousand miles to the east, and roughly four thousand years back in time, to ancient Mesopotamia, the heart of the Fertile Crescent, the cradle of civilization. Situated within a vast, lush stretch of land between the rivers Tigris and Euphrates, in what today is Iraq, a city-state called Babylon played host to a flourishing civilization. Bustling with life and action, it was the trade center of the ancient world.

Babylon, the heart of that dynamic civilization, was a melting pot, an ideal substrate on which myriad belief systems and teachings grew and flourished. The Babylonians practiced many kinds of idol worship. *Sefer HaYashar* [*The Book of the Upright One*] describes the life of the Babylonians at the time, and how they worshipped: "All the people of the land made each his own god in those days—gods of wood and stone. They worshipped them, and they became gods to them. In those days, the king and all his servants, and Terah [Abraham's father] and his entire household, were the first among the worshippers of wood and stone. ... [Terah] would worship them and bow to them, and so did the whole of that generation. Yet, they had abandoned the Lord, who had created them, and there was not a single man in all the land who knew the Lord..."[16]

Still, Terah's son, Abraham, who then still went by the name, Abram, possessed a certain quality that made him unique: he was unusually perceptive, with a scientific zeal for the truth. Abraham was also a caring person, who noticed that his town's people were becoming increasingly unhappy. When he reflected on it, he found that the cause of their unhappiness was the growing egotism and alienation that were taking hold among them. Within a relatively short period of time, they declined from unity and mutual caring, having been "Of one language and of one speech" (Genesis 11:1), into vanity and alienation, saying "Come, let us build us a city, and a tower, with its top in heaven, and let us make us a name" (Genesis, 11:4).

In fact, they were so preoccupied with building their tower of pride that they completely forgot about the people who were once as kin to them. The composition, *Pirkey de Rabbi Eliezer* (*Chapters of Rabbi Eliezer*), one of the *Midrashim* (commentaries) on the Torah (Pentateuch), offers a vivid description not only of the Babylonians' vanity, but also of the alienation with which they regarded one another. The book writes, "Nimrod said to his people, 'Let us build us a great city and dwell in it, lest we are scattered across the earth like the first ones, and let us build a great tower within it, rising toward the heaven ... and let us make us a great name in the land...'

"They built it high ... those who would bring up the bricks climbed up from its eastern side, and those who climbed down, descended from its western side. If a person fell and died, they would not mind him. But if a brick fell, they would sit and cry and say, 'When will another come up in its stead.'"[17]

The attitude of Abraham's countryfolk toward each other troubled him, and he would come there and observe the builders' conduct. *Pirkey de Rabbi Eliezer* continues to describe his observations of their animosity toward each other: "Abraham, son of Terach, went by and saw them building the city and the tower." He tried to speak to them and tell them about the Creator, the governing force of unity he had discovered, to attest that things would be great if only they went by the law of unity, as well. "But they loathed his words," the book describes. Instead, "They wished to speak each other's language," as before, when they were still of one language, "But they did not know each other's language. What did they do? They each took his sword and fought one another to death. Indeed, half the world died there by the sword."[18]

In light of his people's dire situation, Abraham resolved to spread the tenet he had found, regardless of the risks. In his composition, *HaYad HaChazakah* (*The Mighty Hand*), also known as *Mishneh Torah* (*Repetition of the Torah*), the renowned 12th century scholar, Maimonides (the RAMBAM), describes Abraham's determination and efforts to discover life's truths: "Ever since this firm one was weaned, he began to wonder. ...He began to ponder day and night, and he wondered how it was possible for this wheel to always turn without a driver? Who is turning it, for it cannot turn itself? And he had neither a teacher nor a tutor. Instead, he was wedged in Ur of the Chaldeans among illiterate idol worshippers, with his mother and father, and all the people worshipping stars, and he—worshipping with them."[19]

In his quest, Abraham discovered the unity, the oneness of reality, that singular creative force that creates, sustains, and drives all of reality toward its goal. In Maimonides' words, "[Abraham] attained the path of truth ... with his own correct wisdom, and knew that there is one God there who leads... that He has created everything, and that in all that there is, there is no other God but Him."[20]

To understand just what it is that Abraham attained, keep in mind that when Kabbalists speak of God, they aren't referring to an almighty being or to a force that you must worship, please, and appease, which in return rewards devout worshippers with health, wealth, long life, and other worldly benefits. Instead, Kabbalists identify God with Nature, the *whole of Nature*.

Rav Yehuda Ashlag, known as Baal HaSulam (Owner of the Ladder), made several unequivocal statements on the meaning of the term, "God." Succinctly, he explains that God is synonymous with Nature. In the essay, "The Peace," Baal HaSulam writes (in a slightly edited excerpt), "To avoid having to use both tongues from now on—'Nature' and a 'Supervisor'—between which, as I have shown, there is no difference...it is best for us to ... accept the words of the Kabbalists that *HaTeva* [The Nature] is the same...as *Elokim*

[God]. Then, I will be able to call the laws of God 'Nature's commandments,' and vice-versa, for they are one and the same, and we need not discuss it further."[21]

"At forty years of age," writes Maimonides, "Abraham came to know his Maker," the single law of Nature, which creates all things. But Abraham did not keep his discovery to himself: "He began to provide answers to the people of Ur of the Chaldeans, to converse with them and to tell them that the path on which they were walking was not the path of truth."[22] Alas, Abraham was confronted by the establishment, which in his case was Nimrod, king of Babel.

Midrash Rabbah, written in the 5th century C.E., presents a vivid description of Abraham's confrontation with Nimrod, a glimpse into the hardships that Abraham suffered for his discovery and his dedication to the truth. It also provides an amusing peek into Abraham's fervor. "Terah [Abraham's father] was an idol worshipper [who made his living building and selling statues at the family shop]. Once, he went to a certain place and told Abraham to sit in for him. A man walked in and wanted to buy a statue. [Abraham] asked him, 'How old are you?' And the man replied, 'Fifty or Sixty.' Abraham told him: 'Woe unto he who is sixty and must worship a day-old statue.' The man was embarrassed and left.

"Another time, a woman came in with a bowl of semolina. She told him, 'Here, sacrifice before the statues.' Abraham rose, took a hammer, broke all the statues, then placed the hammer in the hands of the biggest one. When his father returned, he asked him, 'Who did this to them?' [Abraham] replied, 'A woman came. She brought them a bowl of semolina and asked me to sacrifice before them. I sacrificed, and one said, 'I will eat first,' and the other said,

'I will eat first.' The bigger one rose, took the hammer, and broke them.' His father said, 'Are you fooling me? What do they know?' And Abraham replied, 'Are your ears hearing what your mouth is saying?'"[23]

At that point, Terah felt that he could no longer discipline his brazen son. "[Terah] took [Abraham] and handed him over to Nimrod [the king, but also the highest spiritual authority in Babylon]. [Nimrod] told him, 'Worship the fire.' Abraham responded, 'Perhaps I should worship the water, which quenches the fire?' Nimrod replied, 'Worship the water!' [Abraham] told him: 'Then perhaps I should worship the cloud, which carries the water?' [Nimrod] told him, 'Worship the cloud!'

"[Abraham] told him: 'In that case, should I worship the wind, which disperses the clouds?' He told him, 'Worship the wind!' [Abraham] told him, 'And should we worship man, who suffers the wind?' [Nimrod] told him: 'You speak too much; I worship only the fire. I will throw you in it, and let the God you worship come and save you from it!

"Haran [Abraham's brother] stood there. He said, 'If Abraham wins, I will say that I agree with Abraham, and if Nimrod wins, I will say that I agree with Nimrod.' When Abraham descended to the furnace and was saved, they asked [Haran], 'Whom are you with?' He told them: 'I am with Abraham.' They took him and threw him in the fire, and he died in the presence of his father. Thus it was said, 'And Haran died in the presence of his father Terah.'"[24]

So Abraham withstood Nimrod, but was expelled from Babylon and left for the land of Haran (pronounced Charan, to distinguish it from Haran, Terah's son). But Abraham did not stop circulating his discovery just because he was exiled from Babylon. Maimonides' elaborate descriptions tell us, "He began to call out to the whole world, to alert them that there is one God to the whole world... He called out, wandering from town to town and from kingdom to kingdom, until he arrived in the land of Canaan...

"And since they [people in the places where he wandered] gathered around him and asked him about his words, he taught everyone...until he brought them back to the path of truth. Finally, thousands and tens of thousands assembled around him, and they are the people of the house of Abraham. He planted this tenet in their hearts, composed books about it, and taught his son, Isaac. And Isaac sat and taught and warned, and informed Jacob, and appointed him a teacher, to sit and teach... And Jacob the Patriarch taught all his sons. He separated Levi and appointed him the head, and had him sit and learn the way of God..."[25]

To guarantee that the truth would carry through the generations, Jacob "commanded his sons not to stop appointing appointee after appointee from among the sons of Levi, so the knowledge would not be forgotten. This continued and expanded in the children of Jacob and in those accompanying them."[26]

ISRAEL—THE DEEPEST CRAVING

The astounding result of Abraham's efforts was the birth of a nation that knew the deepest laws of life, the ultimate Theory of Everything, or in the words of Maimonides: "A nation that knows the Lord was made in the world."[27]

Indeed, Israel is not merely a name of a people. In Hebrew, the word, *Ysrael* (Israel), consists of two words: *Yashar* (straight), and *El* (God). Thus, Israel designates a *mindset* of wanting to discover life's law, a desire to attain or perceive the Creator. In the words of Rabbi Meir Ben Gabai, "In the meaning of the name 'Israel' there is also *Yashar El* [straight to God]."[28] Likewise, in his *Drush* [written sermon] regarding the Traveler's Prayer, the great Ramchal wrote simply, "Israel—*Yashar El.*"

Put differently, Israel is not a genetic ascription or attribution, but rather the name, or direction of the desire that drove Abraham to his discoveries. Genetically, the first Israelites were either Babylonians or members of other nations who joined Abraham's group. The meaning of their name was clear to the ancient Israelites. As Maimonides wrote, they had their teachers, the Levites, and they were taught to follow life's essential laws.

Today, however, we are unaware of the fact that "Israel" actually refers to the desire to know life's basic law, the Creator, and does not allude to a genetic lineage. Nearly 2,000 years of concealment of the truth since the ruin of the Second Temple have practically obliterated the truth that Abraham's discovery was intended for *all* the people in the world, just as Abraham himself intended it for *all* the people in Babylon, and later "began to call out to the whole world," to quote Maimonides.

Through the years, only Kabbalists kept this truth alive. Kabbalists such as Elimelech of Lizhensk,[29] Shlomo Ephraim Luntschitz,[30] Chaim Iben Attar,[31] Baruch Ashlag[32] and many others wrote in plain words: *Ysrael* means *Yashar El* (straight to God).

Moreover, the need to discover this force is more pertinent today than ever. Nothing has changed in Nature since Abraham's time, and the Creator is still the *one* force that creates, governs, and sustains life.

What *has* changed is that today we need true knowledge of the Creator more than ever. In Abraham's time, humanity had numerous other paths to follow besides Abraham's path of truth. Today's social paths, however, are gradually proving themselves ineffective in solving our declining social morals and cohesion.

Indeed, in time, the Babylonian culture dissipated and the people dispersed the world over. Their alienation and social discord, which caused their fall—represented by the fall of the tower—became inconspicuous and unobtrusive. People resettled in new places, bringing with them the Babylonian culture and attitude, unaware that they were carrying their customs of disharmony among them—the seeds of future struggles.

Now that we have a global community, every crisis is on a global scale. The mistakes we make take their toll on the whole world, making Abraham's discovery of a single force paramount, life-saving information that must be added into our calculations and plans if we wish to survive.

UNITY—AND THEREBY, EQUALITY

Today, our only hope is to unite, because unity, as we will see below, is the direction of the force that drives all of life. Our challenge, therefore, is to learn *how* to unite. It is possible and plausible, but in a time of crisis, it will require recognizing life's force and generating a mutual effort to cooperate and collaborate so we can live by this law's dictates.

It should be noted, however, that unity does *not* require parity or similarity. Rather, it requires *disparity*, over which to unite. Today, for example, there are quite a few denominations within the Jewish religion, as well as unaffiliated Jews. Jewish unity would mean that *without* changing our customs, without converging into a single denomination, we would unite and learn to appreciate, and eventually truly care for one another.

If that may seem impossible, consider a family with several children. In a normative family, each child has his or her unique character. More often than not, those characters clash, as our memories of our childhood quarrels with our kin testify. We often think of our brothers and sisters in such terms as, "If he/she weren't my brother/sister, I would never want to be around him/her." But just that fact that we *are* together with our very different kin proves that when there is love, we can unite *above* the differences.

This is precisely what we need to do—unite *above* our differences. In that way we will intensely feel both our diverse, often opposite qualities, and the unity that rides above them. When that happens, we will be able to *use* our differences to the best, as each of us contributes perspectives, ideas, and modes of action that no one else can, thus forming a stronger whole. Just as our bodies need the *different* organs to work together to keep us healthy, we need to remain different, and unite above the differences for a common goal of realizing the role of the Jewish people— to bring the light of unity to the nations.

Following Abraham's departure from Babylon, returning to our previous topic, the city continued to cultivate self-centered abandon. And while there is nothing wrong with pleasure and enjoyment, when it is utterly self-centered, it is eventually self-defeating. The real purpose of life, Abraham found, is to become similar to life's singular force, to experience oneness and unity with all. Our sages call that unity and oneness, *Dvekut* [adhesion], and what they mean by that word is that we should eventually acquire the Creator's qualities and become similar, or even equal to Him.

To quote the words of Rabbi Meir Ben Gabai, "On the part of the *Dvekut* [adhesion] with the forces of the Great Name and His qualities, you cleave unto the Lord your God, for He is His name, and His name is Him, for you are related and similar to Him, and *Dvekut* with Him is the real life."[33] Likewise, the Holy Shlah wrote in *Toldot Adam* [*The Generations of Man*], "Our sages said (*Sotah* 14a), 'And you who cleave unto the Lord,' cleave unto His qualities, and then he is called Adam [man], as in, *adameh la Elyon* [I will be like the most high]."[34]

In the 20th century, Baal HaSulam elaborated extensively on the term, *Dvekut*, defining it as "equivalence of form," meaning acquiring the "form" (qualities) of the Creator. In his "Introduction to the Preface to the Wisdom of Kabbalah," he wrote, "Thus, [the soul] will be fit to receive all the abundance and pleasure included in the Thought of Creation, and will also be in complete *Dvekut* (adhesion) with Him, in equivalence of form.[35]

In the "Introduction to the Book of Zohar," Baal HaSulam adds, "Thus, one buys complete adhesion with Him, for spiritual adhesion is but equivalence of form, as our sages said, 'How is it possible to cleave unto Him? Rather, cleave on to His qualities.'"[36]

In time, as mentioned above, Abraham's group grew into a nation, and the need for a new method of unity arose. Abraham's teachings held as long as everyone in Israel could be taught. But by the time the people of Israel went out of Egypt, they numbered 600,000 men and some three million people altogether. It was impossible to teach all of them in the same manner that one learns from a teacher.

The solution was found at the foot of Mount Sinai. There, at that pivotal point in the history of our people, the most fundamental tenet of our Torah was given, and is given still today, each day and each moment. That tenet, as Rabbi Akiva put it, is "Love your neighbor as yourself."

At the foot of Mount Sinai, explains the great scholar and interpreter, RASHI, we received the Torah, the laws by which we are to unite, because there we agreed wholeheartedly to do so. In his words, "'And Israel encamped there'—as one man with one heart."[37] From that moment on, unity has been the prime asset of the Jewish people, the means by which we attain the Creator, acquire His qualities, and obtain *Dvekut*, equivalence of form (qualities) with Him.

Midrash Tanah De Bei Eliyahu writes, "The Lord said to them, to Israel: 'My sons, have I lacked anything that I should ask of you? And what do I ask of you? Only that you will love one another, respect one another, and fear one another, and that there will be no transgression, theft, and ugliness among you.'"[38]

In time, unity became so crucial as to supersede any other commandment in terms of its importance. It became the one and only key to Israel's spiritual redemption and salvation from its enemies. *Midrash Tanhuma* writes, "If a person takes a bundle of reeds, he cannot break them all at once. But if he takes one at a time, even an infant breaks them. Likewise, Israel will not be redeemed until they are all one bundle."[39]

In the same spirit, *Masechet Derech Eretz Zutah* writes, "Thus would Rabbi Eleazar ha-Kappar say, 'Love peace, and loathe division. Great is the peace, for even when Israel practice idol-worship and there is peace among them, the Creator says, 'I wish not to touch [harm] them,' as it is written (Hosea, 4:17), 'Ephraim is joined to idols; let him alone.' If there is division among them, what is it said about them (Hos, 10:2)? 'Their heart is divided, now they will bear their guilt.'"[40]

And yet, for all that has just been said about the importance of unity, when we look around us it is evident that the majority of people neither wish to unite, nor find any benefit in unity, certainly not with their neighbors, as the tenet dictates. To understand how such a tenet became so paramount to the existence of our people, and now to the entire world, we need to examine the evolution of reality from a different viewpoint than the one science usually takes. We need to look at reality as an *evolution of desires.* When we view reality as such, the reasoning behind the preeminence of the desire to unite, and the consequent acquisition of the quality of the Creator, will become crystal clear. Therefore, the evolution of desires will be the topic of the next chapter.

CHAPTER 2

I Want,
Therefore I Am

Life as an Evolution of Desires

In the previous chapter, we said that the name, *Ysrael* (Israel), combines the words *Yashar* (straight) and *El* (God). We established that the name came about when Abraham assembled people who wished to reach the Creator, to discover God, and who were named "Israel" after that desire. In this chapter we will discuss the formation of desires in general, and the formation of the desire for the Creator, namely Israel, in particular. To do that, we need to examine reality as an evolution of desires.

In 1937, Baal HaSulam published *Talmud Eser HaSephirot* (*The Study of the Ten Sephirot*), a monumental commentary on the writings of the ARI, author of *Tree of Life*. In the commentary, the author goes into great detail explaining that, at the foundation of reality lies the desire to give, which he calls "the will to bestow," which then created the will to receive. This is the reason, explains Baal HaSulam, why our sages testify that "He is good and does good,"[41] and speak of "His desire to do good to His creations."[42]

In Part 1 of *The Study of the Ten Sephirot*, Baal HaSulam explains why the will to bestow necessarily created the will to receive, and why the two desires are the foundation of the whole of Creation. In his words, "As soon as He contemplated the creation in order to delight His creatures, this Light [pleasure] immediately extended and expanded from Him in the full measure and form of the pleasures He had contemplated. It is all included in that thought, which we call 'The Thought of Creation.' ...The Ari said that in the beginning, an upper, simple Light had filled the whole of reality. This means that since the Creator contemplated delighting the creations, and the Light expanded from Him and departed Him, the desire to receive His Pleasures was immediately imprinted in this Light."[43]

To underscore the assertion that the will to bestow, the Creator, created the will to receive in order to give it pleasure, Baal HaSulam labels that section, "The will to bestow in the Emanator necessarily begets the will to receive in the emanated, and it [the will to receive] is the vessel in which the emanated receives His Abundance."[44]

Ashlag was not the first to refer to the will-to-bestow's creation of the will to receive, albeit he did so more implicitly. Rabbi Isaiah HaLevi Horowitz (The Holy Shlah) also wrote that "Since He favored to do good to His creations, He wished to benefit them with the real benefit, as with the matter of the creation of the evil inclination [will to receive, egotism], which is in favor of the creations."[45]

Similar to the two above-mentioned sages, Rabbi Nathan Sternhertz writes in *Likutey Halachot* [*Assorted Rules*], "The Lord magnifies His mercies and kindness, as He wished to benefit His creations in the absolute best of all the best."[46]

Thus, the will to bestow—the Creator—wishes to bestow upon us, His creations, and we are meant to receive that benefit, the bestowal. Yet, what is that benefit, the good we are meant to receive?

In his "Introduction to the Study of the Ten Sephirot," Baal HaSulam writes that the benefit we are meant to receive is the attainment of the Creator, just as Abraham did almost 4,000 years ago. In Ashlag's words, "[upon attainment] one feels the wonderful benefit contained in the Thought of Creation, which is to delight His creatures with His full, good, and generous hand. Because of the abundance of benefit that one attains, wondrous love appears between a person and the Creator, incessantly pouring upon one by the very routes and channels through which natural love appears. However, all this comes to a person from the moment one attains and onwards."[47]

To attain the Creator, we must have similar qualities to His, or in Baal HaSulam's terms, we must obtain "equivalence of form" with Him. In the "Introduction to the Book, *Panim Meirot uMasbirot* [Shining and Welcoming Face]," Ashlag writes, "Thus, how can one attain the Light ... when one is separated and in complete oppositeness of form ... and there is great hatred between them [Creator and person]? ...Therefore, one ... slowly purifies and inverts the form of reception into being in order to bestow. You find that one equalizes one's form with the system of holiness, and the equivalence and love between them returns ... Thus, one is rewarded with the Light ... since he entered the presence of the Creator."[48]

FOUR LEVELS OF DESIRE
SHAPE REALITY

When examining reality from the perspective of the evolution of desires, Kabbalists discovered that the will to receive we've just described contains four distinct levels— still (inanimate), vegetative (flora), animate (fauna), and speaking (human). Ever since the ARI mentioned the division of reality into those four levels back in the 16th century,[49] numerous scholars and Kabbalists have discussed those four levels. The MALBIM (Meir Leibush ben Iehiel Michel Weiser),[50] Rabbi Pinhas HaLevi Horovitz,[51] and the RABaD (Rabbi Abraham Ben David), who wrote, "All of the world's creatures are still, vegetative, animate, and speaking,"[52] are but three of numerous sages referring to reality as consisting of those four levels.

Yet, no sage or scholar is as descriptive as Baal HaSulam. His writings, which he explicitly intended for *everyone* to read and comprehend, systematically and elaborately detail the structure of reality the way Kabbalists and Jewish scholars have perceived it throughout the ages. In his essay, "The Freedom," he explains the structure of the still, vegetative, animate, and speaking desires under the section, "Law of Causality." He explains that all the elements of reality are connected and emerge from one another. In his words, "It is true that there is a general connection among all the elements of reality before us, which abide by the law of causality, by way of cause and effect, moving forward. And as the whole, so is each item for itself, meaning that each and every creature in the world from the four types— still, vegetative, animate, and speaking—abides by the law of causality by way of cause and effect.

"Moreover, each particular form of a particular behavior, which a creature follows while in this world, is pushed by ancient causes, compelling it to accept that change in that behavior and not another whatsoever. This is apparent to all who examine the ways of Nature from a pure scientific point of view and without a shred of bias. Indeed, we must analyze this matter to allow ourselves to examine it from all sides."[53]

THE FOUR LEVELS WITHIN US

What's more, our sages assert, the levels of still, vegetative, animate, and speaking are not exclusive to the outside nature. They exist within each and every one of us, forming the basis of our desires and even the inner structure of each desire. Rabbi Nathan Neta Shapiro writes, "There are four forces in man—still, vegetative, animate, and speaking— and Israel have yet another, fifth part, for they are the Godly speaking."[54]

Baal HaSulam provides a more elaborate explanation of the way these levels of desires work within us: "We distinguish four divisions in the speaking species [humans], arranged in gradations one atop the other. Those are the Masses, the Strong, the Wealthy, and the Sagacious. They are equal to the four degrees in the whole of reality, called 'Still,' 'Vegetative,' 'Animate,' and 'Speaking.'

"The still ... elicit the three properties, vegetative, animate, and speaking. ...The smallest force among them is the vegetative. The flora operates by attracting what is beneficial to it and rejecting the harmful in much the same way as humans and animals. However, there is no individual sensation in it, but a collective force, common to all the plants in the world...

"Atop them is the animate. Each creature feels itself, attracting what is beneficial to it and rejecting the harmful. ...This sensing force in the Animate is very limited in time and space, since the sensation does not operate at even the shortest distance outside its body. Also, it does not feel anything outside its own timeframe, meaning in the past or in the future, but only at the present moment.

"Atop them is the speaking, consisting of an emotional force and an intellectual force together. For this reason, its power in attracting what is good for it and rejecting what is harmful is unlimited by time and place, as it is in the animate. Because of science, which is an intellectual faculty, unlimited by time and place, one can teach others wherever they are in the whole of reality, in the past or in the future, and throughout the generations."[55]

WHERE WE ARE FREE TO CHOOSE

As we just learned from Baal HaSulam, the difference between the speaking level of reality and the other three levels, both in their overall nature and within us, is that we are unlimited by time and place as far as choosing what to draw near us and what to repel. Put differently, in the whole of Nature, the human race is the only species that has freedom of choice. While all other creatures follow Nature's dictates involuntarily, we can *choose* whether to follow them or not. Regrettably, as is evident from today's global crises, when we choose to go against Nature's dictates without full knowledge of the implications of our actions, we suffer harsh consequences for our mistakes.

And since internally we consist of the same four levels, the same rule applies within us, and only those desires and qualities within us that belong to the speaking level are those in which we have freedom of choice.

Within us, the basic, natural desires—for reproduction and continuation of the species, for shelter, and for provision—correspond to the first three levels of desires in Nature—still, vegetative, and animate. The fourth level, "speaking," manifests within us in desires for wealth beyond our needs, power, fame, respect, and knowledge.

The fundamental difference between the three lower levels and the top one is that the lower three exist in every creature on earth. Every creature strives to secure the existence of its species and keep its offspring safe in a fitting shelter. Conversely, the fourth level of desires, which we will roughly define as "desires for wealth, honor, and knowledge," are exclusively human.

Just as in their overall nature, the three lower levels function automatically, according to Nature's dictates. The only faculty in which there is freedom of choice is the speaking level of desires. Therefore, we must first learn the works of our internal nature before we attempt to satisfy the desires of the higher level.

To be able to work with our fourth level of desires properly, we need to know what affects those desires and the purpose of their existence within us. In effect, it is another level of desires within us that "supersedes" all four levels, and which exists only in humans.

A POINT IN THE HEART

This is the level that Rabbi Nathan Shapiro called, "the Godly speaking." It is this desire that drives us to explore how this world runs, what makes it run the way it does, and why. It is this desire that we call "Israel," *Yashar El* (straight to the Creator). In Abraham, that desire appeared as the craving to know "How it was possible for this wheel to always turn without a driver? Who is turning it, for it cannot turn itself?"[56]

Baal HaSulam named that desire to know the Creator, "the point in the heart." In his "Introduction to The Book of Zohar," he explains that the heart can be viewed as the whole of one's desires, and "the point in the heart" is the desire within us that aims toward the Creator.[57] My teacher, Rav Baruch Shalom HaLevi Ashlag (the Rabash), the firstborn son of Baal HaSulam and his successor, explained that the "point in the heart" is the desire called "Israel." In his words, "There is also Israel in a person ... but it is called 'a point in the heart.'"[58]

Now we can see why Abraham was so determined to share what he had found. He knew that human desires were evolving, and he knew that the more they evolve, the more they will turn toward acquiring wealth, power, domination over others, and knowledge. It was clear to him that without acquiring the knowledge of the nature of human desires, people would not be able to manage themselves and their societies properly.

Once Nimrod succeeded in thwarting Abraham's efforts to circulate his knowledge to the Babylonians, that wise man took those who followed him and went out of Babylon to spread his message outward. Indeed, Abraham's legacy for us is that those who understand what he had taught should share the knowledge with whomever is willing to listen. In the words of *The Book of Zohar*, "Abraham dug that well [Beer Sheba]. He founded it because he had taught all the people in the world to serve the Creator. And once he dug it, it is emitting living waters that never cease."[59]

Today's people of Israel are the descendants of Abraham's students, people with points in their hearts, the point of Israel within them. And although that point is now buried under centuries of oblivion, it exists and awaits being rekindled. In the words of the Holy Shlah, "Israel are called the 'Assembly of Israel,' for although below they are parted from one another, still, above, at the root of their souls, they are one unity, and they are congregated, for they are the part of the Lord. The branches [the people of Israel] that wish to return to their roots must follow the example of their roots, meaning unite below as well. When separation is among them, they seemingly cause separation and severance above, see how far the matter extends. Therefore, the whole of the house of Israel must pursue peace and be one, in peace and wholeness, without a flaw, to resemble their Maker [be in equivalence of form with Him], for so is the name of the Lord, 'Peace.'"[60]

Once Israel unite and thus correct themselves, they can fulfill their vocation and be "A light unto the nations" (Isaiah 42:6). In the words of Rabbi Naphtali Tzvi Yehuda Berlin (The *NATZIV* of Volojin), "The main reason why most of us live in exile is that the Lord disclosed to Abraham Our Father that his sons were made to be a light unto the nations, which is impossible unless they are scattered in the exile. So was Jacob, Our Father, when he came to Egypt, where the majority of the people were. By that, His name was made great, when they saw His providence over Jacob and his descendants."[61]

Speaking of the evolution of desires, the human race constitutes the fourth, and highest level of desire, the only one that allows for free choice. But to make the right choices, people need to know how everything works from its root. The Israeli people represent the desire to know the root, and it is therefore their responsibility to study the root, and pass their insights and perceptions on to the rest of humanity. Thus, everyone will know how to make their choices work in their benefit.

To obtain that knowledge, Abraham formed a study method that sages throughout the ages nurtured and developed. The next chapter will depict the evolution of that method which, since the writing of *The Book of Zohar*, has been referred to as "Kabbalah."

CHAPTER 3

Corrections through the Ages

The Evolution of the

Correction Method

In the previous chapter, we said that desires grow from still, to vegetative, to animate, to speaking. We said that this progression occurs both externally, in the overall nature, and internally, within us. We also said that only at the speaking level within us do we have free choice, but that to make choices that are beneficial to us, we must first learn how Nature operates at its root.

Finally, we said that Israel represents the desire to know the root, the Creator, the Maker of all there is, and that Abraham was the first to discover this root. He tried to teach his contemporaries, and today we Jews, the offspring of that desire, must carry on with Abraham's vocation and complete his assignment.

What Abraham discovered was that the only problem with his countryfolk was their growing egos. They were growing too self-centered to maintain a sustainable society. They used to be of "One language and of one speech," but due to their growing egos they became alienated and uncommunicative. They grew so indifferent to one another, so uncaring and preoccupied with self-extolling that, as mentioned in the previous chapter, "If a person fell and died [while building the tower of Babel] they would not mind him. But if a brick fell they would sit and cry and say, 'When will another come up in its stead.'"[62]

Worse yet, Abraham discovered that the growing ego was not about to stop growing. It was an inherent trait in human nature, a distinct characteristic of the speaking level that the ego should constantly grow because it is fueled by envy of others. In his "Introduction to the Book, *Panim Meirot uMasbirot* (Shining and Welcoming Face)," Baal HaSulam writes, "The Creator instilled three inclinations in the masses [people], called 'envy,' 'lust,' and 'honor.' Due to them, the masses develop degree by degree to educe a face of a whole man."[63] In other words, envy is not evil in and of itself, and yet it has to be dealt with, corrected, and aimed in a constructive direction.

THE (NOT NECESSARILY) EVIL INCLINATION

When our sages write about *Yetzer HaRah* (evil inclination), they refer to the way we use envy to hurt others or to benefit at their expense. But if we use the above-mentioned envy, lust, and honor properly, they become our very means of correction. This is why the Holy Shlah wrote, "The worst qualities are envy, hatred, avarice, lust, and so forth, which are the qualities of the evil inclination—the very ones with which he will serve the Creator."[64]

And yet, inherently, we use those inclinations negatively, as it is written (Genesis, 8:21), "The inclination of a man's heart is evil from his youth." Likewise, "There is no evil but the evil inclination," wrote Shimon Ashkenazi,[65] and centuries prior, *Midrash Rabah* established that "People are awash in evil inclination, as it is said, 'For the inclination of a man's heart is evil from his youth.'"[66]

Abraham discovered that of all creations, only people possess an evil inclination. This is why the great Ramchal wrote, "There is no other creation that can do harm like man. He can sin, and rebel, and the inclination of a man's heart is evil from his youth, which is not so with any other creature."[67]

Baal HaSulam writes that the evil inclination is the will to receive.[68] Yet, in previous chapters we said that the will to receive is the whole of Creation, and man constitutes the fourth, and most developed level of the will to receive. Why then is our will to receive the source of all evil?

The problem is that the will to receive on the speaking, human level is not static. It is constantly growing and constantly seeking more. In the words of our sages, "One does not leave the world with half of one's wishes in one's hand, for one who has one hundred desires two hundred; one who has two hundred desires four hundred."[69] Because we constantly seek more, we are always deficient. Likewise, the Holy Shlah says, "One who is not content is always lacking,"[70] and is therefore constantly unhappy and dissatisfied. Looking at our consumer society, we can see that if we succumb to that element in our nature, we will be thrown into a never ending "pleasure-hunt" that cannot end, and that cannot make us happy, either.

Thus, Abraham realized that the evil inclination, the hatred and alienation that appeared among the Babylonians, was causing all the trouble among them, and that there was no hope that this ferment would wind down by itself. However, he also realized that having an intense will to receive was necessary for the completion of the purpose of Creation, for man to achieve *Dvekut* [adhesion, equivalence of form] with the Creator. In the words of Ramchal, completing the quote from above, "But on the other hand, when he [man] is corrected and complemented, he rises above all, and he deserves to adhere [cleave] to Him, and all other creations are dependent upon him."[71]

Therefore, instead of trying to annihilate the evil inclination, Abraham developed a method by which people could correct, or "tame" their inclinations, meaning their egos, and thus benefit from its growth. Once he devised the method, he began to share it with everyone, making no exceptions, as Maimonides testifies, "He began to call out to the whole world."[72]

As we mentioned in the Introduction, Maimonides wrote that Abraham "planted this tenet [that there is one God, one force in the world] in their hearts, composed books about it, and taught his son, Isaac."

However, Abraham's method was suitable only for his contemporaries. It could not, nor was it intended to be suitable for later generations. Because the evil inclination on the speaking level—the will to receive for ourselves, otherwise known as "egotism"—is ever growing and developing, by the time the people of Israel had grown into a nation and went out of Egypt, a new method of correction was required.

The three million or so who went out of Egypt were different from the seventy souls that had entered it two centuries earlier. In Egypt, Israel's will to receive increased tremendously, and required a very explicit set of instructions in order to correct it.

MOSES SAYS, "UNITE!"

The solution came in the form of Moses' Torah, but also with a new precondition for the execution of any correction from that time onward. To receive the Torah, writes the great commentator, RASHI, the people of Israel stood at the foot of Mount Sinai "as one man with one heart."[73] That utter and complete oneness later evolved into one of Israel's most prominent characteristics—mutual guarantee—the noble trait that distinguished Israel from all the nations of the time.

Upon their acceptance of the condition to be as one man with one heart, Israel received the Torah, the instruction, the code of law that would help them tame the ego. With it, they became a society whose every member—man, woman, and child—attained the Creator and lived by the law of mutual guarantee, in equivalence of form with the one God (or force) that Abraham had discovered. The Babylonian Talmud writes, "They checked from Dan to Beer Sheba and no ignoramus [uncorrected person] was found from Gevat to Antipris, and no boy or girl, man or woman was found who was not thoroughly versed in the laws of purity and impurity [corrections according to Moses' law]."[74]

With their newly acquired unity, Israel conquered Canaan—from the word *Keniaa* (surrender)[75]—and turned it into the "Land of Israel"—a place where the desire for the Creator rules. The Temple that Israel established in the land represented their high level of attainment, where they continued to develop and implement Moses' method.

And yet, as our sages write, "The evil inclination is born with man, and grows with him his whole life,"[76] and "The inclination in a man's heart is evil from his youth, and always grows in all the lusts."[77] Still, Moses' method of correction, the laws we call "the Torah," remained intact through the first and second Temples, and even through the exile in Babel.

But as the spiritual decline of Israel continued, the people found it increasingly hard to hold on to their unity and connection with the Creator. As a result, the Second Temple was at a lower spiritual degree (level of connection, or equivalence of form with the Creator) than the first. Kabbalist Rabbi Behayei Ben Asher Even Halua explains, "Since the day when Divinity was present in Israel, upon the giving of the Torah, it did not move from Israel until the ruin of the First Temple. Since the ruin of the First Temple ... it was not permanently present, as during the First Temple."[78]

Eventually, the level of egotism increased in the people of Israel to such an extent that it altogether detached them from each other and from the Creator. Indeed, it was the detachment from each other that caused their detachment from the Creator, from the perception of life's fundamental force. This, in turn, resulted in the ruin of the Second Temple, and the last and longest exile.

In his book, *Netzah Yisrael* [*The Might of Israel*], Rabbi Yisrael Segal describes Israel's fall from grace: "In the Second Temple there was a special virtue, that Israel were not divided in two; there was only unity among them. Therefore, the First Temple was ruined by transgressions that are *Tuma'a* [impurity], and the Lord does not dwell among them in the midst of their *Tuma'a*. But the Second Temple was ruined by unfounded hatred, which revokes their unity, which was their virtue in the Second Temple."[79]

Similarly, the great scholar and poet, Rabbi Abraham Ben Meir Ibn Ezra, wrote, "'And you shall step on their high places,' 'And I will let you ride on the high places of the earth,' and the reason is the unfounded hatred that was present in the Second Temple until it generated the exile over Israel."[80]

THE GREAT FALL, AND THE SEEDS OF REDEMPTION

The exile after the ruin of the Second Temple stemmed from unfounded hatred, but it also served a twofold purpose. The first was that the exile was an incentive to further develop the correction method. Since Moses' Torah no longer sufficed to maintain the nation's spiritual level, it was time to adapt the method to the current condition of the people—being in exile, and more egotistic than during Moses' time. The second purpose of the exile was for Israel to mingle with other nations, to spread the "spiritual gene" throughout the world, and thus enable the correction of the whole of humanity, as Abraham initially intended.

Around the time of the ruin of the Second Temple, two seminal corpuses were composed. One was the Mishnah, and the other was *The Book of Zohar*. The former, along with the Bible, became the foundation of virtually all Jewish wisdom from that day on. The latter, on the other hand, was concealed soon after its writing, and remained hidden for more than a thousand years, until it appeared in the hands of Rabbi Moses de Leon.

The authors of the Mishnah, the Gemarah, and the rest of the writings of our sages provided the exiled people of Israel with guidance on both the spiritual and the physical levels. While the writings narrate spiritual states, they can just as readily be perceived as physical commandments.

Because the laws that our sages instructed originated from spiritual laws, they were applicable in physical life, just as Israel had applied them prior to the ruin of the Temple. In this way, Jews maintained some level of connection with the spiritual level of the past, albeit without the actual attainment of the source and origin of the laws.

Rabbi Menahem Nahum of Chernobyl wrote in regard to Israel's disconnect from the spiritual level and loss of attainment of the Creator: "The reason for the exile is the ruin of the Temple in general and in particular. Israel have [become] so corrupted that they caused the expulsion of the *Shechina* [Divinity] from the general Temple. The particular [personal] Temple is within their hearts ... and through the departure from the particular Temple [Divinity] ... [they] departed from the general Temple and the exile arrived."[81]

In the same spirit, Jonathan Ben Natan Netah Eibshitz wrote, "In the First Temple, Divinity did not move from the Temple because the exile was for a short time. But in the second ruin, which is for a prolonged period of time, the *Shechina* [Divinity] departed altogether."[82]

And while the majority of Jews focused on maintaining a connection with spirituality on the level instructed to them by the sages of the Mishnah and the Gemarah, there have always been those exceptional few who simply could not settle for blind observance of commandments. The questions that drove Abraham to discover the Creator were burning within them; their points in the heart had not been quenched, and they were driven to the deepest of all studies, the wisdom of Kabbalah.

A NEW ERA, A NEW APPROACH

The Kabbalists kept their studies secret. In secret chambers they developed a correction method that would be suitable for *everyone*, whenever needed. In small groups, sometimes alone, they studied and attained, but kept what they had learned and wrote mostly to themselves.

But one day in the 16ᵗʰ century, a young man by the name of Isaac Luria came to the Kabbalist town of Safed in Northern Israel. His arrival marked the start of a new era in the evolution of the correction method. Through his prime student, Chaim Vital, Isaac Luria—known today as the Holy ARI—detailed a completely new approach to the wisdom of Kabbalah. His seemingly technical explanations of the structure of the spiritual system, and his systematic, precise descriptions gradually became the prevailing study method among Kabbalists.

The ARI's prime disciple, Rabbi Chaim Vital, diligently wrote what his teacher had dictated. After the passing of Rabbi Vital, his son began to publish those writings, the most notable of which are *Tree of Life* and *Eight Gates*. In time, those compositions became the foundation of today's predominant method of Kabbalah study, the Lurianic Kabbalah, named after Isaac Luria, the ARI.

PERMISSION TO ENGAGE

Alongside the growing predominance of Lurianic Kabbalah, a gradual emergence from secrecy began as more and more Kabbalists felt the time was ripe to disclose the method by which the world would achieve its final correction.

In his book, *Light of the Sun*, Kabbalist Rabbi Abraham Azulai wrote, "The prohibition from Above to refrain from open study of the wisdom of truth [Kabbalah] was for a limited period, until the end of 1490. Thereafter, it is considered the last generation, in which the prohibition was lifted and permission has been granted to engage in *The Book of Zohar*. And since the year 1540, it has been a great *Mitzva* (commandment, good deed, correction) for the masses to study, old and young. And since the Messiah is bound to come as a result, and for no other reason, it is inappropriate to be negligent."[83]

Although the ARI permitted no one but Chaim Vital to study his teachings, the latter wrote profusely about the importance of studying Kabbalah. "Woe unto the people from the affront of the Torah. They do not engage in the wisdom of Kabbalah, which honors the Torah, for they prolong the exile and all the afflictions that are about to come to the world," he wrote in his introduction to *Tree of Life*.[84]

In the centuries that followed, numerous rabbis, Kabbalists, and scholars stated that the study of Kabbalah was vital for our redemption, and even for the survival of our nation. In the mid-18th century, The Vilna Gaon (GRA), wrote explicitly, "Redemption depends on the study of Kabbalah."[85]

In the early 19th century, Kabbalists began to proclaim that even children should study Kabbalah, explicitly revoking the prohibition to study before the age of forty. The Rabbi of Komarno wrote, "If my people heeded me in this generation, when heresy prevails, they would delve in the study of *The Book of Zohar* and the *Tikkunim* [Corrections], contemplating them with nine-year-old infants."[86]

In the early 1900s, Rav Isaac HaCohen Kook, who later became the first Chief Rabbi of Israel, openly called for the study of Kabbalah, as well as for the return of the Jews to the land of Israel. In *Orot* (*Lights*), he wrote, "The secrets of Torah bring the redemption; they bring Israel back to its land."[87]

On numerous occasions, Rav Kook wrote quite blatantly that every Jew must study Kabbalah, though he rarely used the explicit term and usually referred to it by its known epithets, "the wisdom of truth," "the wisdom of the hidden," "the internality of the Torah," or "the secrets of Torah." In his words, "Before us is an obligation to expand and establish the engagement in the inner side of the Torah, in all its spiritual issues, which, in its broader sense, includes the broad wisdom of Israel, whose apex is the knowledge of God in truth, according to the depth of the secrets of Torah. These days, it requires elucidation, scrutiny, and explanation, to make it ever clearer and ever more expansive among our entire nation."[88]

NOW, ALL TOGETHER

The latest stage in the evolution of the correction method began in the early 1900s and is only now picking up pace. Because we are part of that stage, it is the one that holds the greatest meaning to us.

As discussed in the Introduction, when Abraham first discovered that one force governs and leads the world, he began to spread his knowledge. His aim was to circulate it to *all* the people, none excluded. However, Nimrod, king of Babylon, prevented him from achieving his objective, and Abraham had to leave, finally arriving at the land of Canaan, which he turned into Israel (after the desire to reach *Yashar El*, straight for the Creator).

That objective has not changed throughout the centuries. "Noah was created to correct the world in the state that it was at that time ...and they [his contemporaries] will also receive correction from him," writes Ramchal.[89] Also, in his commentary on the Torah, the Ramchal writes, "Moses wished to complete the correction of the world at that time. This is why he took the mixed multitude, as he thought that thus would be the correction of the world that will be done at the end of correction ... However, he did not succeed because of the corruptions that occurred along the way."[90]

After the ruin of the Second Temple, Kabbalists chose to hide the wisdom from everyone, Jews and non-Jews alike, until the time of the ARI, when they began to feel that the time was ripe to reveal it to all. At that point, they began to teach and circulate the wisdom in a manner that grew more direct and explicit with each generation.

By the start of the 20th century, all inhibitions were off, and Kabbalists openly called for spreading the wisdom and teaching it to all the nations. Rav Kook expressed this mindset very clearly in one of his letters: "I have agreed to disclose all the secrets of the world, since it is time to do unto the Creator, as it is required at this time. Greater and better than I have suffered nationwide slander for such matters, as their pure spirits pressured them for the sake of correcting the generation to speak new words and to reveal the concealed, to which the intellect of the masses was not accustomed."[91]

During World War I, Rav Kook felt compelled to outline the connection he saw between the world's troubles and the rekindling of the spiritual force of Israel through unity. In his book, *Orot* (*Lights*), he wrote, "The construction of the world, which is currently crumpled by the dreadful storms of a blood-filled sword, requires the construction of the Israeli nation. The construction of the nation and the revealing of its spirit are one and the same, and it is one with the construction of the world, which is crumpling in anticipation for a force full of unity and sublimity, and all that is in the soul of the Assembly of Israel."[92]

His contemporary, Baal HaSulam, wrote profusely, and often blatantly, about the need to disclose the wisdom of Kabbalah to everyone, especially today. In his essay, "Messiah's *Shofar*," he wrote, "Know that this is what it means that the children of Israel are redeemed only after the wisdom of the hidden is revealed to a great extent, as it is written in *The Zohar*, 'With this composition, the children of Israel are redeemed from exile.'

"...In my assessment, we are in a generation that is standing at the very threshold of redemption, if we only know how to spread the wisdom of the hidden to the masses.

"...There is another reason for it: We have accepted that there is a precondition for the redemption—that all the nations of the world will acknowledge Israel's law [of bestowal], as it is written, 'And the land shall be full of the knowledge.' It is as in the example of the exodus from Egypt, where there was a precondition that Pharaoh, too, would acknowledge the true God and His laws, and would allow them to leave.

"...You must understand from where the nations of the world would come by such a notion and desire. Know that it is through the dissemination of the true wisdom, so they will evidently see the true God and the true law [of bestowal]. And the dissemination of the wisdom in the masses is called 'a *Shofar* [a clarion, or a festive ram's horn].' Like the *Shofar*, whose voice travels a great distance, the echo of the wisdom will spread throughout the world."[93]

Indeed, the legacy of those spiritual titans has been fulfilled, and today any person who wishes it can study "the wisdom of the hidden" regardless of religion, age, or gender, as it is no longer hidden. As Abraham envisioned, our global Babylon can now study the fundamental law of life that creates it and sustains it, and there are no limitations whatsoever.

But if everything is all right, why is there so much wrong with the world? Why are so many people still suffering, and why does the number of people in plight seem to be growing? If life's fundamental law can be known to all, how come so few know it, especially now that we are at a loss as to how to handle the multiple crises engulfing human society? If that law is the Creator, and can therefore fix everything, why is everyone not rushing to learn it?

To answer these questions we need to understand the routes by which the wisdom spreads, and specifically the role of the Jewish people in the spreading of Kabbalah, and what it means to be a light to the nations. Accordingly, the next chapter will discuss the role of the Jewish people through the eyes of Kabbalah.

CHAPTER 4

A Nation on a Mission

The Role of the Jewish People

"Abraham was awarded the blessing of being as the
stars of the heaven, Isaac, the blessing of the sand,
and Jacob, as the dust of the earth, for the children of
Israel were created to correct the whole of Creation."

Yehuda Leib Arie Altar (ADMOR of Gur),
Sefat Emet [*Truthful Lips*], *Bamidbar* [Numbers].

At the end of the previous chapter we asked, "If everything is all right, why is there so much wrong with the world?" and "If life's fundamental law can be known to all, how come so few know it, especially now that we are we at a loss as to how to handle the multiple crises engulfing human society?" We said that to answer those questions, we need to understand how the knowledge of the law spreads, and how Jews are related to its spreading.

You may recall that in the Introduction, we established that once Abraham discovered that a single force was leading the world, he rushed to tell his countryfolk about his discovery. He posed no preconditions; he wished to share his newfound knowledge with everyone. Alas, neither his king, Nimrod, nor the people were ready to accept the notion that life's governing force is one of bestowal, and that their goal in life, as we said in Chapter 1, is to reveal it through being similar, or even equal to it. The Babylonians of Abraham's time were too preoccupied with building their tower and attempting to defy the laws of Nature.

As Abraham wandered through what is now the Near and Middle East on his way to Canaan, he gathered into his tent, and tenet, all who were able to comprehend his notions and commit to self-transformation from egotism to bestowal. Those people later became the nation of Israel, named so after the desire to reach straight for the Creator.

And yet, life's four levels—still, vegetative, animate, and speaking—are a constant. They must be actualized to the fullest, and all those who physically belong to the speaking level must eventually achieve it spiritually, as well. The fact that not all Babylonians were ready to commit to changing themselves at Abraham's time changes nothing in terms of the final purpose for which the human race exists. Hence, those who were ready and willing to commit became the "guardians" of the knowledge, entrusted with keeping and nurturing it for posterity.

In his essay, "The *Arvut* (mutual guarantee)," Baal HaSulam wrote, "[The Creator said] 'You shall be My *Segula* [remedy/virtue] from among all peoples.' This means that you will be My remedy, and sparks of purification and cleansing of the body shall pass through you onto all the peoples and the nations of the world. The nations of the world are not yet ready for it, and I need at least one nation to start with now, so it will be as a remedy for all the nations."[94]

This quote, coupled with the words of Rabbi Altar, quoted in the beginning of this chapter, "The children of Israel were created to correct the whole of Creation," and joined with the quotations below in this chapter, leaves little doubt as to the view of Jewish spiritual leaders throughout the ages regarding the role for which Jews exist in the world.

When Moses led the people of Israel out of Egypt, he intended first and foremost to pass on to them the law he had learned himself, the law that Abraham had learned before him. His aim was to finish, or at least advance the mission that Abraham had started generations prior. Rav Moshe Chaim Lozzatto, the great Ramchal, wrote about it, "Moses wished to complete the correction of the world at that time. This is why he took the mixed multitude [self-centered people, without corrected desires], as he thought that thus would be the correction of the world that will be done at the end of correction ... However, he did not succeed because of the corruptions that occurred along the way."[95] Despite the difficulties, writes Rabbi Isaac Wildman, "That was Moses' prayer and blessing to the generation of the desert, that they would be the beginning of the correction of the world."[96]

Yet, the world had no wish for correction. The nations were not ready to relinquish self-love and embrace altruism—giving—as their prime quality. So in the meantime, the Israeli nation kept "polishing up" its own correction in wait for the rest of the nations to be ready and willing. In the words of Ramchal, "You should know ... that Creation as a whole will not be completed until the whole of the chosen nation is arranged in the right order, completed in all its decorations, with the *Shechina* [Divinity] adhered to it. Consequently, the world will reach the complete state. ...We must come to a state where the nation is fully complemented in all the required conditions, and the whole of Creation receives its completeness, and then the world will be established permanently in the corrected state."[97]

It follows that the Israeli nation serves as a channel by which correction, namely the quality of bestowal, should reach its intended recipients: the nations of the world. In his eloquent, florid style, Rav Kook details how he sees the role of the Jews regarding the rest of the nations. "As Israel's vocation, being the nation of the Lord, is present, complete, apparent, lasting, and active in the world, it is a valid testimony for the world for all posterity to complement the form of the human race, to keep its characteristics, and to elevate it through the rungs of sanctity appropriate for it ... which the Lord determined. And since our own vocation is ever standing, accompanying the vocation of the whole of Nature—whose law is to complete all creations and bring them to the apex of perfection—we must guard it devoutly for the life of us all, which is kept within it, and for the whole of humanity and its moral development, whose fate depends on the fate of our existence."[98]

As shown in the Introduction to this book, the Rav Kook even goes so far as to say, "The genuine movement of the Israeli soul at its grandest is expressed only by its sacred, eternal force, which flows within its spirit. It is that which has made it, is making it, and will make it still a nation that stands as a light unto nations."[99]

In his book, *Ein Ayah* [*A Hawk's Eye*], the Rav Kook adds further: "Within Israel is a hidden sanctity of elevating the value of life itself through the Divinity that is present in Israel. The national soul of the Assembly of Israel aspires for the most sublime and exalted, to act in life by the most exalted and Godly value, by that same value that will make no person capable of asking, 'What is the purpose of such a life?' having seen the glory and sublimity of its pleasantness and magnificence. With utter completeness will it be completed within the house of Israel, and from it, it will radiate to the earth and to the whole world, 'for a covenant of the people, for a light of the nations.'"[100]

Similarly, Rabbi Naphtali Tzvi Yehuda Berlin (known as "The *NATZIV* of Volojin") wrote, "Isaiah the prophet said, 'I will take you by the hand and keep you; I will give you as a covenant for the people, a light for the nations,' that is, to correct the covenant, which is the faith, for every nation. They will be casting off the faith in idols and will believe in one God. Indeed, the covenant with Abraham our Father had been signed on that matter."[101]

MIX 'N' MINGLE

And yet, how is the correction to flow unto the nations? If the nation of Israel corrects itself, how will that affect any of the other nations?

When Abraham first discovered the Creator, he described it to whomever would listen, and those who joined him became the first corrected people. Those people then went to Egypt and finally emerged from it in much greater numbers, an entire nation. That nation received the Law of Correction, namely the Torah, and corrected itself. In the First Temple, the Jewish nation achieved its highest level of connection with the Creator, as demonstrated in the previous chapter. From there, the nation began to decline until its people were exiled to Babel. When they returned to the Land of Israel, the majority of the Jewish nation *chose* to stay in the diaspora and assimilate.

Indeed, this is how the passing on of the message began. When people who were once corrected—who had transcended self-interest and discovered the Creator—mingled with those who had never had such thoughts, those noble ideas began to spread within the host society, and help instigate more humane thoughts in people's minds. While those were not corrected thoughts deriving from minds that had transcended egotism, the notions of universalism and humanism nevertheless began to take hold in people's minds.

Indeed, during the Renaissance, several renowned scholars maintained that the Greeks had adopted at least some of their concepts from the Jews, in this case specifically from Kabbalah. Johannes Reuchlin (1455-1522), for example, the political counselor to the Chancellor, wrote in *De Arte Cabbalistica* (*On the Art of Kabbalah*): "Nevertheless, his [Pythagoras'] preeminence derived not from the Greeks, but again from the Jews. ...He himself was the first to convert the name Kabbalah, unknown to the Greeks, into the Greek name philosophy."[102]

In 1918, a French pastor, Charles Wagner, was quoted as having written, "None of the resplendent names in history—Egypt, Athens, Rome—can compare in eternal grandeur with Jerusalem. For Israel has given to mankind the category of holiness. Israel alone has known the thirst for social justice, and that inner saintliness which is the source of justice."[103]

More recently, Christian historian, Paul Johnson, wrote in *A History of the Jews*: "The Jewish impact on humanity has been protean. In antiquity they were the great innovators in religion and morals. In the Dark Ages and early medieval Europe they were still an advanced people transmitting scarce knowledge and technology. Gradually they were pushed from the van and fell behind; by the end of the eighteenth century they were seen as a bedraggled and obscurantist rearguard in the march of civilized humanity. But then came an astonishing second burst of creativity. Breaking out of the ghettos, they once more transformed human thinking, this time in the secular sphere. Much of the mental furniture of the modern world too is of Jewish fabrication."[104]

Similarly, In *The Gifts of the Jews: How a Tribe of Desert Nomads Changed the Way Everyone Thinks and Feels*, author Thomas Cahill, former director of religious publishing at Doubleday, describes the Jews' contribution to the world, which, in his view, began during the exile in Babylon. "The Jews started it all," he writes, "and by 'it' I mean so many of the things we care about, the underlying values that make all of us, Jew and Gentile, believer and aethiest, tick. Without the Jews, we would see the world through different eyes, hear with different ears, even feel with different feelings ... We would think with a different mind, interpret all our experiences differently, draw different conclusions from the things that befall us. And we would set a different course for our lives."[105]

Interestingly, some renowned Jewish leaders also wrote about the spreading (and spoiling) of Jewish wisdom after the ruin of the First Temple. Rabbi Shmuel Bernstein of Sochatchov, for example, wrote, "The Greeks had the wisdom of philosophy, which originated from the writings of King Solomon that have come to their possession after the ruin of the First Temple. However, they were spoiled by them with subtractions, additions, and substitutions until false views mingled with them. And yet, the wisdom itself is good, but parts of the bad have mingled with it."[106]

Baal HaSulam wrote similarly in "The Wisdom of Kabbalah and Philosophy": "Sages of Kabbalah observe philosophic theology and complain that they have stolen the upper shell of their wisdom, which Plato and his Greek predecessors had acquired while studying with the disciples of the prophets in Israel. They have stolen basic elements from the wisdom of Israel and wore a cloak that is not theirs."[107]

THE LEGACY OF THE JEWS

The Jews that remained in Babylon after the ruin of the First Temple disappeared, leaving no trace but the notions they had bequeathed to their hosts. Later, when the Second Temple was ruined, the whole of the Jewish people were exiled, and introduced the world to two tenets that were to become the basis of all three predominant, aptly named "Abrahamic" religions: "Love your neighbor as yourself," and "monotheism," meaning that there is only one God, one force governing the world. These notions are paramount to the success of the correction of humanity because when understood correctly, the former defines the mode by which we will achieve correction—through loving others, and not kin, but our neighbors, meaning strangers. The latter defines the essence of our attainment once we are corrected—the singular force of reality.

Accordingly, Professor T.R. Glover from Cambridge University wrote in *The Ancient World*, "It is strange that the living religions of the world all build on religious ideas derived from the Jews."[108] Likewise, Herman Rauschning, a German Conservative Revolutionary who briefly joined the Nazis before breaking up with them, wrote in *The Beast from the Abyss*: "Judaism, nevertheless ... is an inalienable component of our Christian Western civilization, the eternal 'call to Sinai' against which humanity again and again rebels."[109]

The exile of the Jewish people from the Land of Israel was a long process by which Jews, and therefore Jewish values, were gradually absorbed by their host nations. Yosef Ben Matityahu, better known as Josephus Flavius, the Romano-Jewish historian, describes the expulsion of the Jews by the Romans at the beginning of the exile. In *The Wars of the Jews*, Flavius writes, "And as he remembered that the twelfth legion had given way to the Jews, under Cestius their general, he expelled them out of all Syria, for they had lain formerly at Raphanea, and sent them away to a place called Meletine, near Euphrates, which is in the limits of Armenia and Cappadocia."[110]

In Chapter 3, Flavius elaborates, "For as the Jewish nation is widely dispersed over all the habitable earth among its inhabitants, so it is very much intermingled with Syria by reason of its neighborhood, and had the greatest multitudes in Antioch by reason of the largeness of the city, wherein the kings, after Antiochus, had afforded them a habitation with the most undisturbed tranquility."[111]

Today, narrates author Yaakov (Jacob) Leschzinsky in *The Jewish Dispersion*, the Jews have spread the world over, and at a surprising pace. "When we scan the diaspora of Jewry over the entire globe and throughout the entire civilized world," he writes, "we are surprised to see that this nation, which is almost the most ancient in the world, is in truth the youngest in terms of the land under its feet and the sky above its head. Because of the relentless persecutions and forced expulsions, most Jews are but recent newcomers to their respective lands of residence. Ninety percent of the Jewish people have lived in their new homes for no more than fifty or sixty years! (The Jews) are dispersed over 100 lands on all five continents."[112]

Interestingly, their mingling with other nations is precisely what was required to complete Moses' corrections. While it is true that, as long as Israel was apart from other nations, the above-mentioned tenets at the heart of Judaism could not be tainted, it is also true that the Jews had much to gain from their exile among the nations. This is why the Book of Psalms (106:35) tells us that the Jews were exiled to "Mingle themselves with the nations and learn from their actions."

ADAM—THE FIRST MAN, THE COLLECTIVE SOUL

The ARI explains that in truth, we are all parts of a single soul, known to Kabbalists as *Adam HaRishon* (the first man), and to most other folks as Adam. The exile, says the ARI, occurred as a continuation of the correction process. In *Shaar HaPsukim* [*Gate to the Verses*], he wrote, "*Adam HaRishon* [Adam] included all the souls and included all the worlds. When he sinned, all those souls fell from him into the *Klipot* [shells, forms of egotism], which divide into seventy nations. Israel must exile there, in each and every nation, and gather the lilies of the holy souls that had scattered among those thorns, as our sages wrote in *Midrash*

Rabah, 'Why were Israel exiled among the nations? To add foreigners to themselves.'"[113]

In that regard, The *NATZIV* of Volojin wrote, "Its beginning was on Mount Ebal ... but they completed this exalted matter only through exile and dispersion."[114]

It is with good reason that exile is necessary in order to complete the correction of the Jews, and thereafter the entire world. We previously said that when Abraham offered the correction method to his fellow Babylonians, they rejected it because they were too busy being self-indulgent and egotistical. And yet, if we are all parts of one collective soul, as the ARI pointed out, eventually *all of us* will have to achieve correction, by which we will discover the Creator and become like Him. This is the benefit, as described in Chapter 2, that He intended to give humankind.

Thus, Abraham's correction was only the beginning of the process, certainly not its end. In a long and elaborate essay titled, "And They Built Store-Cities," Baal HaSulam writes, "We must also understand what Abraham the Patriarch asked, 'Whereby shall I know that I shall inherit it' (Genesis 15:8)? What did the Creator reply? It is written, 'And He said unto Abram: Know of a surety that your seed shall be a stranger in a land that is not theirs.'"[115] Baal HaSulam explains that with this reply, the Creator promises Abraham that *all* the people will achieve correction through the mingling of the corrected nation—Israel—with the uncorrected nations—in this case represented by Egypt.

Surprisingly, in reply to his question, the Creator promises Abraham exile. And not only that, writes Baal HaSulam, Abraham "...accepted it as a guarantee on the inheritance of the land."[116] Indeed, Abraham knew that a mingling of the desires—represented by the different nations of the world—was necessary in order to complete the correction of humanity. Considering that each of the nations represents a part of Adam's soul, it is necessary for every part of the soul to be introduced to the correction method, and for that part of the soul to eventually adopt it. This is why Israel had to be exiled and spread throughout the world.

As part of the expansion of the correction process in humanity, Abraham went into exile in Egypt, where his tribe had grown into a nation. And when the Israeli nation exiled after the ruin of the First and Second Temples, it introduced the correction method to the entire world.

Although the method has clearly not been adopted by the rest of humanity, it has nevertheless planted the tenets we already mentioned, tenets that form a common basis upon which to begin the correction process as soon as people begin to seek it.

In "The *Arvut* [Mutual Guarantee]," Baal HaSulam details the process by which the Israeli nation corrects itself first, so as to convey the correction to the rest of the nations. In his words, "Rabbi Elazar, son of Rashbi (Rabbi Shimon Bar-Yochai), clarifies this concept of *Arvut* even further. It is not enough for him that all of Israel are responsible for one another, but the whole world is included in that *Arvut*. ...Everyone admits that to begin with, it is enough to start with one nation for the observance of the Torah [law of bestowal] for the beginning of the correction of the world. It was impossible to begin with all the nations at once, as they said that the Creator went with the Torah to every nation and tongue, and they did not want to receive it. In other words, they were immersed in ... self-love ... until it was impossible to conceive in those days to even ask if they agreed to retire from self-love.

"...But the end of the correction of the world will be only by bringing all the people in the world under His work, as it is written, 'And the Lord shall be King over all the earth; in that day shall the Lord be One, and His name one' (*Zechariah*, 14:9) ... 'And all the nations shall flow on to him' (*Isaiah*, 2:2).

"But the role of Israel toward the rest of the world resembles the role of our Holy Fathers toward the Israeli nation. Just as the righteousness of our fathers helped us develop and cleanse to become worthy of receiving the Torah [law of bestowal] ... it is upon the Israeli nation to qualify itself and all the people of the world through Torah and *Mitzvot* [corrections of the egotism], to develop until they take upon themselves that sublime work of love of others, which is the ladder to the purpose of Creation, being *Dvekut* [similarity/equivalence of form] with Him."[117]

Likewise, in his essay, "A Handmaid that Is Heir to Her Mistress," Baal HaSulam writes, "The people of Israel, which has been chosen as an operator of the general purpose and correction ... contains the preparation required for growing and developing until it moves the nations of the worlds, too, to achieve the common goal."[118]

Baal HaSulam and his son, the Rabash, may have been the latest Kabbalists to state that Israel's role in the world is to bring the correction method to the rest of the nations, but they were certainly not the first. Countless rabbis, Kabbalists, and scholars dating back almost to the ruin of the Second Temple, have stated similarly.

Thus, *Midrash Rabah* states that "Israel bring light to the world,"[119] and the Babylonian Talmud added, "The Creator acted with righteousness toward Israel, having dispersed them among the nations."[120] Rabbi Yehuda Altar, the ADMOR of Gur wrote, "Any exile into which the children of Israel enter is only to elicit holy sparks within the nations [similar to Baal HaSulam's above-quoted words]. The children of Israel are guarantors in that they received the Torah in order to correct the whole world, the nations, too."[121]

Similarly, Rabbi Hillel Tzaitlin writes, "If Israel is the one true redeemer of the entire world, it must be fit for that redemption. Israel must first redeem its own soul, the sanctity of its soul, the sanctity of its *Shechina* [Divinity]. ...For that purpose, I wish to establish with this book the 'unity of Israel' ... If founded, the unification of individuals will be for the purpose of internal ascension and an invocation for corrections for all the ills of the nation and the world."[122]

I would like to conclude this chapter with a few more of Baal HaSulam's words, who in a few paragraphs details the purpose of Creation, humanity's entitlement to it, and Israel's role in achieving it. In his words: "Why was the Torah given to the Israeli nation without the participation of all the nations of the world? In truth, the purpose of Creation applies to the entire human race, none excluded. However, because of the lowliness of the nature of Creation [being egotistical] and its power over people, it was impossible for people to understand, determine, and agree to rise above it. They did not demonstrate the desire to relinquish self-love and come to equivalence of form, which is adhesion with His attributes, as our sages said, 'As He is merciful, be you merciful, as well.'

"Thus, because of their ancestral merit [the examples set by Abraham, Isaac, and Jacob], Israel succeeded ... and became qualified and sentenced themselves to a scale of merit [corrected themselves to become like the Creator]. Each and every member of the nation agreed to love his fellow man [which is how they achieved the correction].

"...However, the Israeli nation was to be a 'transition,' meaning that to the extent that Israel cleanse themselves by keeping the Torah [laws of bestowal], they pass their power on to the rest of the nations. And when the rest of the nations also sentence themselves to a scale of merit [correcting themselves by relinquishing egotism], the Messiah [final correction] will be revealed. This is because the role of the Messiah is not only to qualify Israel to the ultimate goal of adhesion with Him, but to teach the ways of God [bestowal] to all the nations, as it is written, 'And all nations will flow onto Him.'"[123]

CHAPTER 5

Pariahs

The Roots of Anti-Semitism

Throughout history, never has a nation been more persecuted than the Jews. Throughout history, never has a nation survived every single persecution *and* emerged stronger every time.

The apparent indestructibility of the Jews raised many questions, albeit more among non-Jews than among Jews, as the Jews were too preoccupied with survival. Renowned German writer, Johann Wolfgang von Goethe, expressed his bewilderment over the Jews' tenacity in his book, *Wilhelm Meisters Lehrjahre* [*Wilhelm Meister's Apprenticeship*]: "Every Jew, no matter how insignificant, is engaged in some decisive and immediate pursuit of a goal... It is the most perpetual people on earth."[124]

Similar to Goethe, Cambridge professor, T.R. Glover, underlines the conundrum of Jewish existence in *The*

Ancient World: "No ancient people have had a stranger history than the Jews. ...The history of no ancient people should be so valuable, if we could only recover it and understand it. ...Stranger still, the ancient religion of the Jews survives when all the religions of every ancient race of the pre-Christian world have disappeared ... The great matter is not 'What happened?' but 'Why did it happen?' Why does Judaism live?"[125]

Likewise, Ernest van den Haag, professor of Jurisprudence and Public Policy at Fordham University, wrote, "In a world where Jews are only a tiny percentage of the population, what is the secret of the disproportionate importance the Jews have had in the history of Western culture?"[126]

The French mathematician, physicist, inventor, and philosopher, Blaise Pascal, was fascinated with the Jewish people's antiquity. In his book, *Pensees*, he wrote, "This people are not eminent solely by their antiquity, but are also singular by their duration, which has always continued from their origin till now. For, whereas the nations of Greece and of Italy, of Lacedaemon, of Athens and of Rome, and others who came long after, have long since perished, these ever remain, and in spite of the endeavors of many powerful kings who have a hundred times tried to destroy them, ...they have nevertheless been preserved."[127]

Indeed, as countless renowned individuals throughout the ages have noted, the Jews cannot be annihilated. The Jews have a mission to fulfill, and until they do, Nature, God, the Creator, Yahweh, or however you may choose to call Him, will not let it happen. And yet, as long as Jews continue to avoid assuming their intended task, they certainly can, have been, and will be tortured and slaughtered *almost* to extinction. To unearth the roots of the Jewish *Via Dolorosa* through history, we need to journey back in time to the onset of Creation.

In Chapter 2 we noted that the Creator has but one desire—to do good to His creations, namely us humans. But because we currently have no perception of Him, we cannot receive from Him.

When we want to give a present to a friend, we approach that friend and give it. There must be contact between the giver and the receiver. Just so, for Him to give to us, the Creator and Creation must connect. And upon connection, as we quoted Baal HaSulam, "One feels the wonderful benefit contained in the Thought of Creation, which is to delight His creatures with His full, good, and generous hand. Because of the abundance of benefit that one attains, wondrous love appears between a person and the Creator, incessantly pouring upon one by the very routes and channels through which natural love appears. However, all this comes to a person from the moment one attains and onwards."[128]

This, we said in Chapter 2, arouses the need for "equivalence of form," that is, to be like the Creator, having a nature of giving. Regrettably, the vast majority of us have no desire for it; we vehemently resent giving unless we have some underlying profit, an ulterior motive to do so. RASHI, the great commentator on the Bible, wrote that the verse, "The inclination of a man's heart is evil from his youth" (Genesis 8:21), means that "As soon as one is shaken out of his mother's womb, He [the Creator] plants in him the evil inclination," which, as said in Chapter 3, is egotism, the desire to receive for ourselves.

Therefore, considering that the Creator is benevolent and that we are the opposite, the clash between man and God seems inevitable. How can we ever attain Him if He has made us inherently opposite from Him? The remedy to egotism lies in what we described earlier as "the point in the heart." That thirst to understand what life is about, and what makes the world go around (and it is not money), is the yearning that enabled Adam, Abraham and his progeny, Moses, and the entire nation that arose out of the pariahs from Babylon, to develop a correction method that turns the evil inclination into goodness.

SYMBOLS OF AN INNER CLASH

One may argue whether or not the Bible, the Old Testament, is a genuine historic documentation of events. But the great sages of Israel throughout the ages had no concern for the historic relevance of the Bible. Rather, they viewed it as an allegory that depicts internal, spiritual processes that one experiences along the path of correction. To them, Nimrod, king of Babylon, represents *meridah* [Hebrew: rebellion], defiance against the quality of bestowal, the Creator; Pharaoh stands for the epitome of the evil inclination, and so does Haman, albeit at a later stage in one's spiritual development.

This is why RASHI interprets the Babylonian Talmud as follows: "His name was Nimrod for he *himrid* [incited] the whole world against the Lord."[129]

Regarding Pharaoh, Maimonides explains affectionately, "You should know, my son, that Pharaoh, king of Egypt, is in fact the evil inclination."[130] Similarly, Elimelech of Lizhensk, author of *Noam Elimelech* (*The Pleasantness of*

Elimelech), simply wrote, "...Pharaoh, who is called 'the evil inclination.'"[131]

Rabbi Jacob Joseph Katz added depth to the distinction regarding Pharaoh. He explained that the words, "Pharaoh had let the people go" (Exodus 13:17), designate the stage in one's spiritual development when a person breaks free from the evil inclination's heavy shackles. In his words, "'And when Pharaoh had let the people go'—when one's organs exit the authority of the evil inclination, as during the exodus from Egypt, they came out of the forty-nine gates of *Tuma'a* [impurity, egotism] toward sanctity [bestowal]."[132]

Within the same book, Rabbi Katz adds his insights regarding Haman: "Haman's instruction to make a gallows fifty cubits high is the counsel of the evil inclination."[133] Similarly, Rabbi Jonathan Eibshitz writes in his book *Yaarot Devash* [*Honeycombs*] of "Haman, who is the evil inclination..."[134]

More recently, Kabbalists and Jewish scholars began to feel that time was of the essence and that the Age of Correction was nearing. They began to add implicit, and sometimes explicit calls to action to their words. Thus, Rav Yehuda Ashlag, sensing that the application of the correction method was urgently needed, made a direct link between overcoming the evil inclination and the way it must be achieved today—through unity. In an essay titled, "There Is a Certain People," Baal HaSulam tells us, "'There is a certain people scattered abroad and dispersed among the peoples.' Haman said that in his view, we [Haman's people] will succeed in destroying the Jews because they are separated from one another, so our strength against them will certainly prevail, because this [separation among them] causes separation between man and God."[135] That is, the egoism of the Jews separates them from the quality of bestowal, the Creator, so the strength of the ego, the evil inclination, "will certainly prevail." "This is why," continues Baal HaSulam, "Mordecai went to correct that flaw, as it is explained in the verse, 'The Jews gathered...' to gather themselves together, and to stand up for their lives. This means that they had saved themselves by uniting."[136]

We can therefore conclude that whether or not Nimrod, Pharaoh, Balak, Balaam, or Haman actually existed is of lesser importance. What *is* important is that the *traits* portrayed by these characters exist within us, and the Bible only allegorically narrates the stages by which we can overcome them.

When we prevail over these qualities of egotism, we are rewarded with redemption—the quality of bestowal, the equivalence of form with the Creator. And because the Creator desires to do good to us, once we have corrected these traits within us, they will haunt us no more, since we have been redeemed from egotism and acquired His quality of bestowal.

If any of these examples of egotism lived today, we would certainly categorize them as anti-Semites of the worst kind. To that effect, the Rav Kook made a forbidding (and true) prediction while drawing a direct link between modern anti-Semites and biblical ones. In a rather unorthodox statement he writes, "Amalek, Petlura [Ukrainian leader suspected of being anti-Semitic], Hitler, and so forth, awaken for redemption. One who did not hear the voice of the first *Shofar* [a symbol of a call for redemption], or the voice of the second ... for his ears were blocked, will hear the voice of the impure *Shofar*, the foul [non-kosher] one. He will hear against his will."[137]

TWO WAYS—ONE BLISSFUL, ONE PAINFUL

The state of complete redemption—the attainment of the Creator by all of humanity—is mandatory. Baal HaSulam says that there are two ways by which we can achieve it: the way of Torah, when we voluntarily adopt the law of bestowal as our way of life, or the way of suffering, whereby reality compels us to nevertheless adopt the Law of Bestowal as our way of life.[138]

As compulsory as the words of those two contemporary sages may sound, they rest on a sound basis. The Talmud writes, "Rabbi Eliezer says, 'If Israel repent, they are redeemed. If not, they are not redeemed.' Rabbi Yehoshua said to him, 'If they do not repent, they are not redeemed, but the Lord will set up over them a king whose decrees are as harsh as Haman's, Israel will repent, and He will reform them.'"[139]

Even that momentous occasion at the foot of Mount Sinai, when we collectively received the Torah with a spectacular audio-visual show, was apparently not as joyous or as festive as has been described. The Talmud tells us that the circumstances were such that there was not much else we could do other than receive it. In today's terminology, we would say that the Creator gave us an offer we could not refuse: "It is written, 'And they stood at the bottom of the mountain.' Rav Dimi Bar Hama said that it means that the Lord had forced the mountain over Israel like a vault, and said unto them: 'If you accept the Torah [Law of Bestowal], very well, but if not, there will it be your grave.'"[140]

Indeed, no one said that it is easy having the primogeniture. But the Jews, the descendants of Abraham's clan, are just that. They were the first to attain the purpose of Creation; hence, it is naturally up to them to lead the way for the rest of humanity. As long as we avoid that undertaking, we will encounter rejection by all the nations.

THE WORLD'S MEDICS

Imagine you have found a series of exercises that heal cancer and prevent it from ever returning. Imagine you had told the world about it, as did Abraham in Babylon, but you were rejected because the exercises were monotonous and tiring, and no one really felt unwell.

Now imagine that years later, billions of people around the world have cancer. They vaguely remember that you said you had a cure, and in their desperation they turn to you, begging you to save their lives. But you have forgotten all about it. You know the cure exists, you know that many people said it was a powerful remedy (*Segula*), but since you feel strong and healthy, you see no reason why you should relearn those exercises, much less teach them to billions of people. Can you imagine how the world would feel about you, what people would think, and what they would do?

This is precisely where we Jews stand in relation to the world. The world is beginning to feel unwell, and people are beginning to search for a way out of their plight. They know we are the chosen people, and that we are the ones meant to bring redemption. People may not know that redemption entails changing their nature to bestowal, but they know that redemption is desirable.

Such verses from the New Testament as "You worship what you do not know; we worship what we know, for salvation is from the Jews,"[141] and "What advantage has the Jew? ...Great in every way. First of all, they were entrusted with the oracles of God,"[142] are only two of countless mentions of the Jews' unique position and role, as depicted in Christian writings. When we do not carry out our mission, we inadvertently draw toward us anger and hatred, which translate into what we now regard as anti-Semitism.

That we are different and unique is documented in history, in the pages of our scriptures, in those of Christianity and Islam, and in the writings of myriad scholars and statespersons. Below are a few of the countless excerpts from well-known individuals expressing their views on the uniqueness of Jews:

Winston Churchill, Prime Minister of the UK during World War II: "Some people like the Jews, and some do not. But no thoughtful man can deny the fact that they are, beyond any question, the most formidable and the most remarkable race which has appeared in the world."[143]

Lyman Abbott, an American Congregationalist theologian, editor, and author: "When sometimes our own unchristian prejudices flame out against the Jewish people, let us remember that all that we have and all that we are we owe, under God, to what Judaism gave us."[144]

Huston Smith, a religious studies professor in the United States, author of *The World's Religions*, which has sold more than two million copies: "There is a striking point that runs through Jewish history as a whole. Western civilization was born in the Middle East, and the Jews were at its crossroads. In the heyday of Rome, the Jews were close to the Empire's center. When power shifted eastward, the Jewish center was in Babylon; when it skipped to Spain, there again were the Jews.

When in the Middle Ages the center of civilization moved into Central Europe, the Jews were waiting for it in Germany and Poland. The rise of the United States to the leading world power found Judaism focused there. And now, today, when the pendulum seems to be swinging back toward the Old World and the East rises to renewed importance, there again are the Jews in Israel..."[145]

Leo Tolstoy, the Russian novelist, author of *Anna Karenina*: "What is the Jew?...What kind of unique creature is this whom all the rulers of all the nations of the world have disgraced and crushed and expelled and destroyed, persecuted, burned, and drowned, and who, despite their anger and their fury, continues to live and to flourish. What is this Jew whom they have never succeeded in enticing with all the enticements in the world, whose oppressors and persecutors only suggested that he deny (and disown) his religion and cast aside the faithfulness of his ancestors?!

"The Jew is the symbol of eternity. ...He is the one who for so long had guarded the prophetic message and transmitted it to all mankind. A people such as this can never disappear. The Jew is eternal. He is the embodiment of eternity."[146]

Indeed we *are* the symbol of eternity, as Tolstoy said, because the Creator's quality of benevolence is in our "spiritual genes." And yet, we will not be left in peace until, as in the example with the cancer and the healing exercise, we consciously elevate ourselves to the spiritual level and raise the whole of humanity immediately thereafter.

As has been stated and quoted above, now is the time of the general correction. At such a time, events become inclusive, global. Such was the case with World War I, and even more so with World War II, the atrocities of which are embedded in our collective memory to remind us who we are, and what we are meant to accomplish.

To avoid such cataclysms in the future, we need to take a closer look at some suggestions and statements given prior to, and following the Holocaust. The next chapter will highlight those statements and their pertinence to our lives today. Once we know what has been said, we will be able to appreciate what we need to do to help ourselves and help the world.

CHAPTER 6

Expendable

Contemporary Anti-Semitism

I n Chapter 1, we said that Abraham discovered that human nature's inherent egotism is on a constant trend of expansion. The method he devised was not intended to curb that egotism because he knew this was impossible, as man was created to receive boundlessly. His only question, therefore, was how to receive that intended bounty. Abraham discovered a method where, by studying and striving to unite, people rose to a new level of perception. Here, they acquired the nature of the Creator—benevolence—and could therefore receive that boundless pleasure without becoming overindulgent and dangerous to themselves or the environment.

The exodus from Egypt and the formation of the nation of Israel marked a five-century stage of formation. During that time, Israel went from being a group made of family and students into an entire nation whose goal was to attain the Creator.

While attempting to rise to the highest spiritual level, the Hebrews never retreated from their original intention to offer their perceptions to the whole of humanity. This was to be their contribution to the nations, the "light" they were meant to give them. Through the generations, that gift of "light" is what the nations have been trying to receive from the Jews, and the lack of which has been the cause of our afflictions by the nations.

In the prologue to his book, *A History of the Jews*, Christian historian and novelist, Paul Johnson, eloquently describes the questions that drove Abraham to his discoveries, the same questions that drive humanity to this day. Johnson portrays his reverence for the Jews' ability to discover the answers to those questions, live by their consequent laws, and their efforts to teach them to others. In his words, "The book gave me the chance to reconsider objectively, in the light of a study covering nearly 4,000 years, the most intractable of all human questions: what are we on earth for? Is history merely a series of events whose sum is meaningless? Is there no fundamental moral difference between the history of the human race and the history, say, of ants? Or is there a providential plan of which we are, however humbly, the agents? No people has ever insisted more firmly than the Jews that history has a purpose and humanity a destiny. At a very early stage in their collective existence they believed they had detected a divine scheme for the human race, of which their own society was to be a pilot. They worked out their role in immense detail. They clung to it with heroic persistence in the face of savage suffering. Many of them believe it still.

Others transmuted it into Promethean endeavors to raise our condition by purely human means. The Jewish vision became the prototype for many similar grand designs for humanity, both divine and man-made. The Jews, therefore, stand right at the centre of the perennial attempt to give human life the dignity of a purpose."[147]

THE WRITING ON THE WALL

And yet, by the onset of the 20th century, the Jews had grown so far from their intended vocation that, by and large, they became either utterly preoccupied with meticulous observation of the practical commandments, forgetting or rejecting their internal meaning, or fully absorbed in worldly, material desires, forgetting or rejecting their irrevocable vocation. At a time when egotism spiked to levels that threatened world peace, neither avenue was desirable, and some of the nation's great spiritual leaders began to warn that time was of the essence, that we had to wake up to our mission and carry it out before calamity unfolded.

The great scholar humanist, and Kabbalist, Rav Avraham Yitzhak HaCohen Kook, desperately tried to alert the Jews to the growing anti-Semitism. He warned them that no country would be safe for them, and that Israel was the only secure option. In retrospect, the content of his premonition is alarming, giving us a glimpse into the depth of such people's clarity of vision.

The treatise in which he entreated with the Jews to come to Israel was called, "The Great Call for the Land of Israel." Note not only his plea, but also his warning regarding the Jews' possible future in their homelands: "Come to the land of Israel, delightful brothers, come to the land of

Israel. Save your souls, the souls of your generations, and the soul of our entire nation. Save it from desolation and oblivion; save it from decay and degradation; save it from all the uncleanness and wickedness, from every trouble and plight that might befall it in all the countries of the nations without exception.

"'Come to the land of Israel!' We shall call out with a loud and terrible voice, with the sound of thunder and a great voice, a voice that stirs storm and quakes the heaven and the earth, a voice that tears every wall in the heart. Run for your lives and come to the land of Israel. The voice of the Lord is calling us, His hand is stretched out to us, His spirit is in our hearts, and He assembles us, encourages us, and compels us all to call out loud with a terrible and mighty voice: 'Our brothers, children of Israel, dear beloved brothers, come to the land of Israel. Assemble one by one, wait not for formal words and orders; wait not for permits from renowned ones. Do what you can, flee and gather, come to the land of Israel. Pave the way for our beloved and oppressed nation. Show it that its way is paved already, stretched out before it. It must not rest; it has nothing to demand; it has not many ways and routes. There is one way before it, and this is the one it shall march; it is the one it *must* march, specifically to the land of Israel.'"[148]

The Rav Kook was not alone in his concern. In Poland, a brilliant young *dayan* (Orthodox judge) in Warsaw—at the time the biggest and most prominent Jewish community in Europe—Rav Yehuda Ashlag, who later became a renowned commentator on *The Book of Zohar*, did not settle for publicly announcing that all Jews must flee Europe. He arranged for the purchase of 300 wooden shacks from

Sweden and a place for them to be erected in the Land of Israel (which was then called "Palestine").

Alas, his plan was thwarted by opposition from leaders of the Jewish congregation in Poland. The tragic consequence of Ashlag's failure to bring his fellow Jews with him was that of all the Jews who contemplated coming with Ashlag, only Ashlag and his family eventually emigrated. The rest of the families remained in Poland and perished in the Holocaust.[149]

Both the Rav Kook and Rav Ashlag (Baal HaSulam) expressed how they perceived the rise of Nazism to power, and specifically Hitler. Keep in mind that Rav Kook died in 1935, four years *before* World War II even broke out. Below are Rav Kook's edited words (to make them more reader friendly, due to the length of the text and its anachronistic style), followed by the words of Baal HaSulam.

The prophet predicted a great *Shofar* of redemption. [A *Shofar* is a ram's horn used for festive blowing, but also a clarion.] We pray *specifically* for the blowing of a great *Shofar*. There are several degrees in a *Shofar* of redemption—a great *Shofar*, a medium *Shofar*, and a small *Shofar*. The *Shofar* of the Messiah is considered the *Shofar* of *Rosh Hashanah* [Hebrew New Year's Eve]. The *Halachah* [Jewish law] distinguishes between three degrees in the *Shofar* of *Rosh Hashanah*: 1) A *Shofar* of *Rosh Hashanah* that is made of a ram's horn; 2) In retrospect, all *Shofars* are kosher; 3) A *Shofar* from an impure beast, as well as a *Shofar* from beasts of idol-worship of a non-kosher gentile. However, if one has blown such a *Shofar*, one has done one's duty.

It is permitted to blow any *Shofar*, kosher or not, as long as one does not bless over it, and the degrees explained in the law of the *Shofar* of *Rosh Hashanah* coincide with the degrees of the *Shofar* of redemption.

Yet, what is a *Shofar* of redemption? By the term, "Messiah's *Shofar*," we refer to the awakening and thrust that causes the revival and redemption of the people of Israel. It is this awakening that assembles the lost and the rejected, and brings them to the mountain of holiness in Jerusalem.

Throughout the generations, there have been those in Israel who felt the awakening that stems from the desire to do God's will, which is Israel's complete redemption [bringing all of Israel to the quality of bestowal]. This is the fine and great *Shofar*, the people's desire to be redeemed.

Sometimes the desire dwindles and the zeal for sublime notions of holiness is not as fervent. However, the healthy human nature remains, and sets off a simple desire in the nation to establish its rule in its land. That natural desire is the ordinary, medium *Shofar*, which is present everywhere. That, too, is still a kosher *Shofar*.

However, there is a third degree to the *Shofar* of the Messiah, which is nonetheless comparable to the *Rosh Hashanah Shofar*: it is the small, non-kosher *Shofar*, which is blown only if a kosher *Shofar* cannot be found.

Thus, if the zeal for holiness and yearning for redemption that derives from it have all but vanished, and if the natural national desire for a national life has diminished, too, and no kosher *Shofar* is found by which to blow, *the enemies of Israel come and blow into our ears for our redemption.* They force us to heed the *Shofar*'s voice; they warn and rattle in our ears, and give us no rest in exile.

[This part is quoted in full.] "Thus, the *Shofar* of a foul beast becomes the Messiah's *Shofar*. Amalek, Petlura [Ukrainian leader suspected of being anti-Semitic], Hitler, and so forth, awaken for redemption. One who did not hear the voice of the first *Shofar*, or the voice of the second ... for his ears were blocked, will hear the voice of the impure *Shofar*, the foul [non-kosher] one. He will hear against his will. ...While there is redemption in that whip, as well, in the plight of the Jews, one must not bless over such a *Shofar*.[150]

Baal HaSulam, too, made several references to Nazism, including how he believed it could be overturned. In his words, "It is impossible to bring down Nazism unless by a religion of altruism."[151] Note that when Baal HaSulam speaks of "religion of altruism," he does not mean that we should perform certain rituals or observe particular conducts. Rather, by "religion of altruism" he means that one has *changed one's nature* into that of altruism. At the same time, people will choose whether or not to stay in their formal denominations, regardless of this transformation.

Baal HaSulam also disputes the notion that Nazi Germany was a once-in-history event. It may have been the first, but he believed that unless we do what we must, it will not be the last. In his words, "It turns out that people mistakenly think that Nazism is only an offshoot of Germany ... all the nations are equal in that, and it is utterly futile to hope that the Nazis will perish with the victory of The Allies, for tomorrow the Anglo-Saxons will embrace Nazism..."[152]

In light of the spike in anti-Semitism worldwide, it would be wise to seriously consider the words of these wise men. After all, we can evidently see that anti-Semitism has not vanished, nor has Nazism or the call to do away with the Jews.

WHAT THEY NEED AND WHAT WE GIVE

On the face of it, it seems as though the world is ungrateful for the contributions made by Jews to the benefit of humanity in science, education, economy, sociology, psychology, and virtually every realm of life. However, that ostensible ingratitude should serve as an indication that what we are giving is not necessarily what they need from us.

In fact, people do acknowledge the uniqueness of the Jewish people, but it is we who misuse that uniqueness by giving what we want to give, instead of what they want to receive.

To better understand what the world needs from us, we should look at some of the more damning and poignant documents written about Jews. A great example of such a document is Henry Ford's (founder of the Ford Motor Company) infamous book, *The International Jew— The World's Foremost Problem*. While still making gross generalizations, the book often establishes points that are well worth considering. For that, however, we must put aside our affront, and truly look into Ford's arguments (emphases in italics are the editor's): "Every Jew ought to know also that in every Christian church where the ancient prophecies are received and studied, there is a great revival of interest in the future of the Ancient People. It is not forgotten that certain promises were made to them regarding their position in the world, and it is held that these prophecies will be fulfilled. *The future of the Jew ... is intimately bound up with the future of this planet,* and the Christian church in large part ... sees a Restoration of the Chosen People yet to come. If the mass of the Jews knew how understandingly and sympathetically all the prophecies concerning them are being studied in the Church, and the faith that exists that these prophecies will find fulfillment and that they will result in *great Jewish service to society at large,* they would probably regard the Church with another mind."[153]

Earlier in the book, Ford writes, "The whole prophetic purpose with reference to Israel seems to have been the moral enlightenment of the world through its agency."[154] And in another place, he adds, "Society has a large claim against [the Jew] that he ... begin to fulfill [what], in a sense, his exclusiveness has never yet enabled him to fulfill—the ancient prophecy that through him all the nations of the earth should be blessed."[155]

John Adams, second President of the United States, also commented on what he believed the Jews have given to the world. In his words, "The Hebrews have done more to civilize men than any other nation. If I were an atheist, and believed in blind eternal fate, I should still believe that fate had ordained the Jews to be the most essential instrument for civilizing the nations. If I were an atheist of the other sect, who believe, or pretend to believe that all is ordered by chance, I should believe that chance had ordered the Jews to preserve and propagate to all mankind the doctrine of a supreme, intelligent, wise, almighty sovereign of the universe, which I believe to be the great essential principle of all morality, and consequently of all civilization."[156]

Samuel Langhorne Clemens, better known by his pen name, Mark Twain, does acknowledge the Jewish distinction in all realms of human engagement, but he, too, ends up pondering the source of that preeminence: "...If statistics are right, the Jews constitute but one percent of the human race. It suggests a nebulous dim puff of stardust lost in the blaze of the Milky Way. Properly, the Jew ought hardly to be heard of, but he is heard of, has always been heard of. He is as prominent on the planet as any other people, and his commercial importance is extravagantly out of proportion to the smallness of his bulk. His contributions to the world's list of great names in literature, science, art, music, finance, medicine, and abstruse learning are also away out of proportion to the weakness of his numbers. He has made a marvelous fight in this world, in all the ages; and had done it with his hands tied behind him. He could be vain of himself, and be excused for it.

"The Egyptian, the Babylonian, and the Persian rose, filled the planet with sound and splendor, then faded to dream-stuff and passed away; the Greek and the Roman followed, and made a vast noise, and they are gone. Other people have sprung up and held their torch high for a time, but it burned out, and they sit in twilight now, or have vanished. The Jew saw them all, beat them all, and is now what he always was, exhibiting no decadence, no infirmities of age, no weakening of his parts, no slowing of his energies, no dulling of his alert and aggressive mind. All things are mortal but the Jew; all other forces pass, but he remains. What is the secret of his immortality?"[157]

And finally, there are those who not only recognize that Jews are special in the spiritual sense, more than in the corporeal one, but even detail the essence of that spirituality: unity. Such was the case of Prime Minister of the United Kingdom during World War II, Sir Winston Churchill. In *Churchill and the Jews*, author Martin Gilbert quotes Churchill: "The Jews were a lucky community because they had that corporate spirit, the spirit of their race and faith. [Churchill] would not ... ask them to use that spirit in any narrow or clannish sense, to shut themselves off from others ... far from their mood and intention, far from the counsels that were given them by those most entitled to advise. That personal and special power which they possessed would enable them to bring vitality into their institutions, which nothing else would ever give. [Churchill sincerely believed that] A Jew cannot be a good Englishman unless he is a good Jew."[158]

We can therefore see that what the nations want from the Jews is not excellence in science, finance, or any of the other realms mentioned in the quotes above. What the world needs from us is *spirituality*, namely, the *ability to connect to the Creator*. This is the one thing that we had possessed, and which no other nation has, had, can, or is intended to possess unless we rekindle it within us and pass it on as a light for the nations. As long as we refrain from carrying out that mission, the nations will by and large consider us expendable, if not downright injurious, and certainly, as Ford stated, "The world's foremost problem."

OUT OF FAVOR

To demonstrate how expendable the world might think we are, consider the following facts: In 1938, Adolf Hitler was willing to send German and Austrian Jews out to whomever would have them. No one did. Hitler declared that he could "only hope and expect that the other world, which has such deep sympathy for these criminals [Jews], will at least be generous enough to convert this sympathy into practical aid. We [Nazi Germany], on our part, are ready to put all these criminals at the disposal of these countries, for all I care, even on luxury ships."[159]

And yet, the nations unanimously declined to take in the Jews. In July of 1938, representatives of most of the countries of the free world gathered in Évian-les-Bains, a resort town on the Southern shore of the pristine Lake Geneva, in France. Their goal was to discuss, and find solutions to the "Jewish problem," namely the Jews who wished to flee from Germany and Austria before it was too late. The German and Austrian Jews were very hopeful about the conference. They believed the participating countries would genuinely seek to help them and offer them a safe haven. They were bitterly disillusioned.

While the conference delegates did express empathy for the plight of the Jews under the Nazi regime, they made no commitments and offered no solutions. Instead, they portrayed the conference as a mere beginning, which was never continued. Diplomatically, the delegates stated that, "The involuntary emigration of people in large numbers has become so great that it renders racial and religious problems more acute, increases international unrest, and may seriously hinder the processes of appeasement in international relations."[160]

However, since the conference, convened by U.S. President Franklin D. Roosevelt, assembled under a precondition that "no country would be forced to change its immigration quotas, but would instead be asked to volunteer changes,"[161] to no one's surprise, the resolutions of the conference offered the desperate Jews of Germany and Austria very little hope.

According to Yad Vashem, World Center for Holocaust Research, Documentation, Education and Commemoration, Israel's official memorial to the Jewish victims of the Holocaust, "As the conference proceeded, delegate after delegate excused his country from accepting additional refugees. The United States delegate, Myron C. Taylor, stated that his country's contribution was to make the German and Austrian immigration quota, which up to the time had remained unfilled, fully available. The British delegate declared that their overseas territories were largely unsuitable for European settlement, except for parts of East Africa, which might offer possibilities for limited numbers. Britain itself, being fully populated and suffering unemployment, also was unavailable for immigration; and he excluded Palestine from the Evian discussion entirely. The French delegate stated that France had reached 'the extreme point of saturation as regards admission of refugees.' The other European countries echoed this sentiment, with minor variations. Australia could not encourage refugee immigration because, 'as we have no real racial problem, we are not desirous of importing one.' The delegates from New Zealand, Canada, and the Latin American nations cited the Depression as the reason they could not accept refugees. Only the tiny Dominican Republic volunteered to contribute large, but unspecified areas for agricultural colonization."[162]

A few months after the conference, the doors had closed and the fate of Europe's Jewry was sealed.

ANTI-SEMITISM IN DISGUISE

While the atrocities of the Holocaust helped the Jewish settlement in Israel win recognition and compassion, and the Jewish State of Israel was founded in 1948, it did very little to uproot anti-Semitism. Instead, anti-Semitism acquired a new form: "anti-Zionism."

There are those who argue that anti-Zionism differs from anti-Semitism. Baal HaSulam, on the contrary, asserts that hatred of Jews is just that, regardless of the form it takes. In his succinct and forward style, he writes, "It is a fact that Israel is hated by all nations, whether for religious reasons, racial reasons, capitalistic reasons, communistic reasons, or cosmopolitan reasons. It is so because the hatred precedes all reasons, but each [person] merely resolves one's loathing according to one's own psychology."[163]

But as is often the case with Jews, our best advocates come from among the nations. About a year after the 1967 Six Day War, American social writer, Eric Hoffer, who was awarded the Presidential Medal of Freedom, and in whose honor the Eric Hoffer Award was established, published an open letter in the *Los Angeles Times*. Perhaps it was the fact that Mr. Hoffer was not Jewish that enabled him to write so candidly about the state of the Jews in the world.

"The Jews are a peculiar people," he begins. "Things permitted to other nations are forbidden to the Jews. Other nations drive out thousands, even millions of people, and there is no refugee problem. Russia did it, Poland and Czechoslovakia did it. Turkey threw out a million Greeks and Algeria a million Frenchman. Indonesia threw out heaven knows how many Chinese and no one says a word about refugees. But in the case of Israel, displaced Arabs have become eternal refugees. Everyone insists that Israel must take back every single Arab.

"[British historian] Arnold Toynbee calls the displacement of the Arabs an atrocity greater than any committed by the Nazis.

"Other nations, when victorious on the battlefield, dictate peace terms. But when Israel is victorious, it must sue for peace. Everyone expects the Jews to be the only real Christians in this world.

"Other nations—when they are defeated—survive and recover, but should Israel be defeated, it would be destroyed. Had Nasser [President of Egypt during the 1967 Six Day War] triumphed last June he would have wiped Israel off the map and no one would have lifted a finger to save the Jews. No commitment to the Jews by any government, including our own [US government], is worth the paper it is written on.

"There is a cry of outrage all over the world when people die in Vietnam or when two Negroes are executed in Rhodesia. But when Hitler slaughtered Jews no one remonstrated with him. The Swedes, who are ready to break off diplomatic relations with America because of what we did in Vietnam, did not let out a peep when Hitler was slaughtering Jews. They sent Hitler choice iron ore and ball bearings, and serviced his troop trains to Norway.

"The Jews are alone in the world. If Israel survives it will be solely because of Jewish efforts, and Jewish resources. Yet at this moment Israel is our only reliable and unconditional ally. We can rely more on Israel than Israel can rely on us. And one has only to imagine what would have happened last summer had the Arabs and their Russian backers won the war to realize how vital the survival of Israel is to America and the West in general.

"I have a premonition that will not leave me; as it goes with Israel so will it go with all of us. Should Israel perish the holocaust will be upon us."[164]

Another remarkable example of sympathy relates this time to the debate over whether one who opposes Zionism also opposes Jews. Below are the extraordinary words of Reverend Martin Luther King Jr., who, in a letter to a friend, makes the case for the Jews in general, and for the Jewish state in particular, in such compelling eloquence that Israel's Foreign Ministry can only envy.

Here is Martin Luther King's "Letter to an Anti-Zionist Friend": "...You declare, my friend; that you do not hate the Jews, you are merely 'anti-Zionist.' And I say, let the truth ring forth from the high mountain tops, let it echo through the valleys of G-D's green earth: When people criticize Zionism, they mean Jews—this is G-D's own truth.

"Anti-Semitism, the hatred of the Jewish people, has been and remains a blot on the soul of mankind. In this we are in full agreement. So know also this: anti-Zionist is inherently anti-Semitic, and ever will be so.

"Why is this? You know that Zionism is nothing less than the dream and ideal of the Jewish people returning to live in their own land. The Jewish people, the Scriptures tell us, once enjoyed a flourishing Commonwealth in the Holy Land. From this they were expelled by the Roman tyrant, the same Romans who cruelly murdered our L-RD. Driven from their homeland, their nation in ashes, forced to wander the globe, the Jewish people time and again suffered the lash of whichever tyrant happened to rule over them.

"...How easy it should be, for anyone who holds dear this inalienable right of all mankind, to understand and support the right of the Jewish People to live in their ancient Land of Israel. All men of good will exult in the fulfillment of G-D's promise that His people should return in joy to rebuild their plundered land. This is Zionism, nothing more, nothing less.

"And what is anti-Zionist? It is the denial to the Jewish people of a fundamental right that we justly claim for the people of Africa and freely accord all other nations of the Globe. It is discrimination against Jews, my friend, because they are Jews. In short, it is anti-Semitism.

"The anti-Semite rejoices at any opportunity to vent his malice. The times have made it unpopular, in the West, to proclaim openly a hatred of the Jews. This being the case, the anti-Semite must constantly seek new forms and forums for his poison. How he must revel in the new masquerade! He does not hate the Jews, he is just 'anti-Zionist!'

"My friend, I do not accuse you of deliberate anti-Semitism. I know you feel, as I do, a deep love of truth and justice and revulsion for racism, prejudice, and discrimination. But I know you have been misled—as

LIKE A BUNDLE OF REEDS

others have been—into thinking you can be 'anti-Zionist' and yet remain true to those heartfelt principles that you and I share. Let my words echo in the depths of your soul: When people criticize Zionism, they mean Jews—make no mistake about it."[165]

Approximately since the turn of the century, we have been witnessing a rise in anti-Semitism throughout the world. An executive report issued by the U.S. State Department confirms that "The increasing frequency and severity of anti-Semitic incidents since the start of the 21st century ... has compelled the international community to focus on anti-Semitism with renewed vigor. ...In recent years, incidents have been more targeted in nature with perpetrators appearing to have the specific intent to attack Jews and Judaism."[166]

In some cases, there is anti-Semitism where there are no Jews at all! A report titled, "Anti-Semitism without Jews," by writer, editor, and photographer Ruth Ellen Gruber, details the prevalence of anti-Semitism in Europe, even where there are no Jews whatsoever. According to Gruber, "I've been asked to discuss the phenomenon of 'anti-Semitism without Jews' in historical terms, but also within the context of what has been called the 'new anti-Semitism' that has manifested itself in Europe—and, indeed, elsewhere ... I have to say that I am not really comfortable with the term 'new anti-Semitism.' As the London Jewish Chronicle put it in an editorial last year, anti-Semitism is a 'light sleeper,' easy to rouse. It is also often referred to as a virus, a protean virus which, like disease-causing viruses in the human body, is able to mutate in an opportunistic fashion to defeat whatever defenses or anti-bodies have been built up against it. It has done so many times, even in post-Holocaust countries whose Jewish population is practically invisible. And it is doing so now."[167]

Perhaps less surprising, but still unsettling, is the phenomenon of Malaysia's formal anti-Semitism. On October 6, 2012, Robert Fulford of the Canadian *National Post*, published a story about Malaysia's anti-Semitism, stating that in Malaysia, "Politicians and civil servants devote a surprising amount of time to thinking about Israel, 7,612 km [4730 miles] away. Sometimes they appear to be obsessed by it. Malaysia has never had a dispute with Israel, but the government encourages the citizens to hate Israel and also to hate Jews whether they are Israelis or not."[168]

"Few Malaysians have laid eyes on a Jew; the tiny Jewish community emigrated decades ago," writes Fulford. "Nevertheless, Malaysia has become an example of a phenomenon called 'Anti-Semitism without Jews.' Last March, for instance, the Federal Territory Islamic Affairs Department sent out an official sermon to be read in all mosques, stating that 'Muslims must understand Jews are the main enemy to Muslims as proven by their egotistical behavior and murders performed by them.'

"In Kuala Lumpur, it's routine to blame the Jews for everything from economic failures to the bad press Malaysia gets in foreign ('Jewish-owned') newspapers."[169]

Evidently, even the Holocaust did not change people's minds regarding the Jews. As I wrote in the Foreword to this book, "since around the turn of the century, anti-Semitism has been on the rise once more, this time the world over. The specter of the hatred of the Jews has taken root worldwide." The sympathy we had had after World War II was evidently short-lived, and now a new, even more wide-ranging wave of anti-Semitism than ever is on the rise.

In Chapter 2 we quoted Rabbi Nathan Shapiro's words: "There are four forces in man—still, vegetative, animate, and speaking—and Israel have yet another, fifth part, for they are the Godly speaking."[170] If we keep in mind that the goal of creation is for *everyone* to achieve that last degree, which only Israel has, and which Abraham had intended to give to *all* his Babylonian countryfolk, we will see that what we need to give the world is one, very simple thing— the quality of bestowal, embodied in the maxim, "Love your neighbor as yourself." When egotism thrives throughout the world, this quality is the only remedy that can offset a global clash of unprecedented proportions.

The Jews, therefore, must rekindle that trait within them as individuals and as a nation, and lead the way for the whole of humanity. Indeed, acquiring the quality of bestowal is tantamount to the revelation of the Creator through equivalence of form. Regrettably, as the next chapter will show, we often attempt to avoid that mission, either because we are unaware of it, or because we have no desire for it. Thus, instead of embracing our vocation and paving the way to the light for the whole of humanity, we try to assimilate ourselves to extinction and to be like all other nations.

CHAPTER 7

Mingle Bells

To Be Jewish,

or Not to Be Jewish,

That Is the Question!

One of the most important prayers on *Yom Kippur* (Day of Atonement) is known as *Maftir*[171] *Yonah* (Jonah), during which the entire book of Jonah is read. The story of Prophet Jonah symbolizes more than anything the ambivalence that our people feels toward its role in the world.

Admittedly, it is not a pleasant task to be the eternal wet blanket. Even within our own nation, prophets rarely had it easy or were treated with gratitude for saving us from calamity and affliction. Yet, prophets always carried out their tasks. They were compelled to do so by the dread of the torment that would otherwise befall their unsuspecting brethren, so they could not keep quiet.

Jonah tried his hardest to avoid his mission. He hid his identity as a Hebrew and boarded a ship that sailed to

LIKE A BUNDLE OF REEDS

Tarshish, away from Nineveh, where the Creator had told him to prophesy. But as we know, the Creator found him in the ship and the sailors discovered his identity and threw him overboard, where he was tormented in the bowels of a fish. Finally, after he repented (praying from the bowels of the fish), he went to Nineveh and prophesied. Thanks to Jonah's repentance, the residents of Nineveh learned about the correction required of them, executed it, the city was spared, and its people were pardoned.

Interestingly, Nineveh was not a Hebrew city. It was the most populous city in the Assyrian Empire and a prosperous trade hub. Yet, the Lord commanded Jonah to prophesy to them so they might better their ways and avoid affliction. This, again, indicates that the path of correction and attainment of the Creator was not meant for Jews alone, but for all of humanity. How symbolic it is that we read this story on the most Jewish day of the year—*Yom Kippur*, The Day of Atonement.

Thus, Jonah's story epitomizes the dilemma of Jewish people throughout the generations. On the one hand, we are the chosen people, intended to show the way to the light to all the nations. On the other hand, we insistently and futilely try to avoid our fate because the message of mutual guarantee and unity that we bring is unpleasant to the listener's ego, as we are all born self-centered and want to remain that way.

When the Jews returned from the exile in Babel to build the Second Temple, those who remained behind assimilated so thoroughly among their host nations that they disappeared entirely. *The Jewish Encyclopedia*[172] writes that once freed from captivity in Babylon, Jews gradually spread to Syria, Egypt, and Greece—mainly as slaves, but rather inadequate ones, so they had no trouble being ransomed and freed.

"Besides," informs *The Jewish Encyclopedia*, "owing to the close solidarity, which is one of the lasting traits of the Jewish race, they had no difficulty finding coreligionists willing to pay the amount of their ransom."[173] However, continues the encyclopedia, "The Jews thus freed, instead of returning to Palestine, usually remained in the land of their former slavery, and there, in conjunction with their brethren in faith, established communities. According to the formal testimony of Philo (*Legatio ad Caium*, §23), the Jewish community in Rome owed its origin to released prisoners of war."[174] From Rome, the Jews went on to spread through the rest of Europe.

Once liberated from Babylon, however, the minority of the Hebrews who did return to the Land of Israel became what is now known as "the Jewish people." After the ruin of the Second Temple, they, too, wished to assimilate. Yet, unlike their former brethren, the Jews who were exiled from Jerusalem and Judea were never allowed by the nations to mingle to the point of disappearance. Had that happened, the purpose for which the Jews exist, namely the revelation of the Creator to the rest of the nations, would have been defeated.

Perhaps this is why notable historians and theologians wrote similar words to those of Professor Emeritus of Judaism at the University of Wales, Dan Cohn-Sherbok: "The paradox of Jewish life is that hatred and Jewish survival have been interrelated for thousands of years, and that without anti-Semitism, we may be doomed to extinction."[175]

Indeed, despite often desperate attempts to mingle and assimilate, we were always reminded of our heritage and were either harshly driven back into Judaism, or remained as outcasts in our new religions. Today, many Jews are still trying to assimilate into their host cultures, but for all the apparent success in some countries, history shows that it has never succeeded, and the Jewish task mandates that it never will.

Particularly notable examples of Jewish assimilation and rejection took place in 14th and 15th century Spain, and in Germany, before and during World War II and the Holocaust, resulting in the extermination of virtually the entire European Jewry. Although much has been said and written about those two epochs in Jewish history, it is worthwhile to note some similarities that could point to a repetitive trend we might use as an augury. We will address those periods one at a time, and conclude with reflections on today's most prominent Jewry outside of Israel—that of the United States.

SPAIN, THE TRAGIC LOVE STORY

Josephus Flavius wrote of the warm welcome with which the expatriates from Judea were received in Syria and Antioch after their expulsion by the Romans. Jews were "very much intermingled," he wrote, and lived "with the most undisturbed tranquility."[176] He also wrote about how the Roman Emperor, Titus Flavius, "expelled them out of all Syria."[177] In *Antiquities of the Jews*, he quoted Greek geographer Strabo as saying, "This people has already made its way into every city, and it is not easy to find any place in the habitable world which has not received this nation and in which it has not made its power felt."[178]

The vacillating manner in which Jews are first warmly welcomed, then rejected, then welcomed again, then repelled once more, if not altogether destroyed, has repeated itself numerous times since the ruin of the First Temple.[179] As just pointed out above, the exiled Jews of the First Temple who chose to spread out of Babylon, once given freedom, managed to assimilate to the point of disappearance. However, many, if not most of the Jews who were exiled after the ruin of the Second Temple are still recognized as such, at least by heritage if not by some level of practice.

There have been many attempts to convert Jews into Islam or Christianity, and they themselves often wished to, and actively attempted to convert. And yet, for the most part, those attempts either failed or were only marginally successful.

Professor and researcher of Jewish History at the University of Wisconsin, Norman Roth, details both the en-masse attempts of Jews to convert, and the tragic consequences that resulted from those attempts. In *Jews, Visigoths, and Muslims in Medieval Spain: cooperation and conflict*, he writes, "In the fourteenth and fifteenth centuries, thousands of Jews converted, chiefly of their own free will and not under any duress, to Christianity. The role of these *conversos* [Jews who converted to Christianity] in society led to fierce hostility against them in the fifteenth century, finally resulting in actual warfare. Racial anti-Semitism emerged, for the first time in history of a large scale, and the *limpieza de sangre* [purity of blood] statutes were enacted [distinguishing 'pure' Old Christians from those with Muslim or Jewish ancestors]. Finally, the Inquisition was revived amidst false charges of the 'insincerity' of the *conversos*, and many were burned. None of this, however, had anything to do with the Jews, who for the most part continued their lives, and their normal relations with Christians, as before."[180]

Indeed, not only were the Jews who maintained their faith not harmed, but they even nurtured a unique bond with their Spaniard hosts. According to Roth, "So unusual, one may say unique, was the nature of that relationship [between Jews and Christians] that a special term is used in Spanish for it, a term which has no precise translation in other languages, *convivencia* [roughly meaning, "living together in affinity"]. In truth, the real extent of *convivencia* in medieval Christian Spain has not yet been fully revealed."[181]

Roth's study stresses that as long as Jews remained loyal to their heritage and did not try to assimilate in foreign cultures, they were welcome to stay, or were at least left in peace. And specifically in Spain, at times the warmth and intensity of the relationship truly resembled a love story, complete with all the trials and tribulations that great love stories exhibit. However, when Jews tried to mingle with other nations and become like them, those nations would reject them and force them back into Judaism, or *force* them to convert, but in a derogatory and coercive manner.

Jane S. Gerber, an expert on Sephardic history at the City University of New York, eloquently details the extent to which Spain's Jews and *conversos* immersed themselves in Spain's secular and cultural life (emphases are the editor's). "Deeply rooted in the Iberian peninsula since the dawn of their dispersion," writes Gerber, "these Jews had fervently nurtured a love for Spain and felt a deep loyalty to her language, regions, and *traditions* (...) In fact, *Spain had been considered a second Jerusalem.*

"When King Ferdinand and Queen Isabella's decree of expulsion was promulgated on March 31, [1492] ordering the 300,000 Jews of Spain to leave within four months, the Sephardim reacted with shock and disbelief. Surely, they felt, the *prominence of their people in all walks of life*, the sheer longevity of their communities (...) and the *presence of so many Jews and Christians of Jewish ancestry (conversos) in the inner circles of the court, municipalities, and even the Catholic church* could provide protection and avert the decree.

"...Spanish Jews were especially proud of their long line of poets, whose ... songs continued to be recited. Their philosophers had been influential even among the scholars of the West, their innovative grammarians had earned a lasting place as pioneers of the Hebrew language, and their mathematicians, scientists, and innumerable physicians had won acclaim. The resourcefulness and *public service of Sephardic diplomats also filled the annals of many Muslim kingdoms. In fact, they had not just resided in Spain; they had co-existed side by side with Muslims and Christians, taking the notion of living together (la convivencia) with utmost seriousness.*

"The experience of Sephardim raises the issue of acculturation and assimilation as no other Jewish community has. For many centuries, *Jewish civilization borrowed freely from the surrounding Muslim culture.* ...When persecutions overwhelmed the Sephardim in 1391 and they were offered the choice of conversion or death, the numbers of converts outnumbered the considerable number of martyrs. The very novelty of this mass conversion, unique to Jewish experience, has induced scholars to seek causality in the *high degree of acculturation attained by the Sephardim.*"[182]

And yet, it was not the acculturation that caused the Spaniards to turn against the Jews. It was rather the Jews' abandonment of social cohesion and mutual guarantee, traits that had (for the most part) won them the unconscious esteem of their host nations. "Medieval commentators especially," continues Gerber, "were fond of placing the blame for *the breakdown of communal discipline* upon Jewish acculturation, and some of the greatest modern Jewish historians, such as Itzhak Baer, have cited in addition the corrosive impact of Averroist philosophy and the cynicism of Spain's assimilated Jewish courtier class. But in the wave of mass conversions and *the sharp communal conflicts, it was not just the philosophers who succumbed in the face of persecution.*"[183] Rather, the entire community suffered.

Thus, conscious or not, the Jews were afflicted, and were eventually expelled from Spain because they had become too disunited, forgetting about the powers and benefit that unity can bring them, and which our sages have taught our forefathers for generations. *The Book of Zohar* wrote about the panacea of unity: "Because they are of one heart and one mind ... they will not fail in doing that which they purport to do, and there is no one who can stop them."[184]

But *The Book of Zohar*, which resurfaced in Spain just a few centuries prior to the expulsion, could not save the Jews. They were simply too spiritually and culturally assimilated to unite, and carry out their intended role of being a light to the nations. And since they would not adjust their course of their own accord, Nature's Law of Bestowal, the Creator, did it through their surroundings, the Christian Spaniards, to whom the Jews looked up.

English classicist, author, and professor at Cambridge University, Michael Grant, observed the Jews' inability to mingle: "The Jews proved not only unassimilated, but inassimilable. ...The demonstration that this was so proved one of the most significant turning points in Greek history, owing to the gigantic influence exerted throughout subsequent ages by their religion, which not only survived intact, but subsequently gave birth to Christianity."[185]

Similarly, 18th century bishop, Thomas Newton, wrote about the Jews: "The preservation of the Jews is really one of the most signal and illustrious acts of divine Providence... and what but a supernatural power could have preserved them in such a manner as none other nation upon earth hath been preserved. Nor is the providence of God less remarkable in the destruction of their enemies, than in their preservation... We see that the great empires, which in their turn subdued and oppressed the people of God, are all come to ruin... And if such hath been the fatal end of the enemies and oppressors of the Jews, let it serve as a warning to all those, who at any time or upon any occasion are for raising a clamor and persecution against them."[186]

Because, as mentioned in Chapter 4, Jews represent in our world the part of Adam's soul that achieved unity of hearts and thus connection with the Creator, and because their spiritual role is to spread that unity and resulting connection to the rest of the nations, the nations reject the Jews' attempts to become like them. It is not a conscious act of choice, but a compulsive drive that comes upon them from the very thought of Creation. This only rarely surfaces to the awareness of the perpetrators of affliction, but they unfailingly execute it.

One remarkable incident of the thought of Creation rising to the perpetrator's awareness took place on a fateful and tragic night in 1492. In *The Jew in the Medieval World: A Sourcebook: 315-1791*, scholar of Jewish history, Rabbi Jacob Rader Marcus details the events he discovered had taken place. "The agreement permitting them [Jews] to remain in the country [Spain] on the payment of a large sum of money was almost completed when it was frustrated by the interference of a prior who was called the Prior of Santa Cruz. [Legend relates that Torquemada, Prior of the convent of Santa Cruz, thundered, with crucifix aloft, to the King and Queen: 'Judas Iscariot sold his master for thirty pieces of silver. Your Highness would sell him anew for thirty thousand. Here he is, take him, and barter him away.']"[187] What happened next illustrates that whatever happens, the Jews are obliged to be what they are, and do what they must. "Then the Queen gave an answer to the representatives of the Jews, similar to the saying of King Solomon [Proverbs 21:1]: 'The king's heart is in the hand of the Lord, as the rivers of water: He turneth it whithersoever He will.' She said furthermore: 'Do you believe that this comes upon you from us? The Lord hath put this thing into the heart of the king.'"[188]

Indeed, the Jews were expelled not because they had stopped being of economic value to the Spaniards. Jews had been recognized as an economic asset for centuries. In fact, when they were forced out of Spain, many of them fled to Turkey, who welcomed them precisely *because* of their contribution to the economy of their hosting country. Accordingly, the Ottoman Sultan, Bayezid II, was so delighted at the Jews' expulsion from Spain and their arrival in Turkey that it is reported that he "sarcastically thanked Ferdinand for sending him some of his best subjects, thus impoverishing his own lands while enriching his (Bayezid's)."[189] Another source reports that "when King Ferdinand who expelled the Jews from Spain was mentioned in [Bayezid's] presence, he said: 'How can you consider King Ferdinand a wise ruler when he impoverished his own land and enriched ours?'"[190]

Time and again, we find that it is not our astuteness that grants us the nations' favor. Rather, it is our unity, for our unity projects on them the light, or rather the delight that they were intended to receive through us in the thought of Creation. In the words of the writer and thinker, Rabbi Hillel Tzaitlin, "If Israel is the one true redeemer of the entire world, it must be fit for that redemption. Israel must first redeem its own soul ... But how will it redeem its soul? ...Will the nation, which is in ruins both in matter and in spirit, become a nation made entirely of redeemers? ...For that purpose, I wish to establish with this book the 'unity of Israel' ... If founded, the unification of individuals will be for the purpose of internal ascension and an invocation for corrections for all the ills of the nation and the world."[191]

Indeed, even if we claim every Nobel Prize from here till Doomsday, for all the benefit that scientific achievements bring to humanity, we will not gain credit, but aversion. We may produce the finest physicians, the most illustrious economists, the most brilliant scientists, and the most innovative entrepreneurs, but until we produce the light, the power we elicit through unity, the nations will never accept us, and we will never justify our existence on this planet.

NAZI GERMANY:
HORROR BEYOND WORDS

As pointed out earlier in the chapter, another notable example of Jewish assimilation and rejection took place in Germany, preceding and during World War II. The horrific consequences of the unfolding that took place in Germany have been thoroughly discussed and analyzed, and there is not much to add concerning what took place. What we should point out, however, is the repetition of the culprits that affected the Spanish Inquisition and ultimate expulsion from Spain.

Historically, German Jewry did not enjoy the freedom and affinity with its host duchies and cities as did the Jews in Spain. Instead, for centuries they would wander from city to city, reside where permitted, always under harsh restrictions and discrimination, and at times, such as during the Crusades, suffering persecution, expulsion, and even massacres.

And yet, starting from the 16th century, in tandem with the Renaissance, the Jews in Germany enjoyed relative peace. While they did not receive equal status or citizenship at any of their hosting cities or duchies, they were left to run their own lives relatively uninterrupted and separate from the rest of the German society.

"Behind their ghetto walls," writes Sol Scharfstein in *Understanding Jewish History: From Renaissance to the 21st Century*, "following their own traditions and their own way of life, Jews weathered the storms of the centuries that followed, the struggles between Christians, between the church and princes, and the wars and revolutions set off by the new conditions and new ideas.

"...[Pope] Paul IV argued that it was foolish for Christians to be friendly to a people who had not accepted Christ as their savior. In a papal bull he decreed that Jews living in areas controlled by the church were to be confined in the ghettos. They would be permitted to leave the ghetto in daytime to go to work, but forbidden to be outside at other times. The ghetto gates were to be closed at night and on Christian holidays," and the gates were "...guarded by non-Jews watchmen who controlled the entry and exit of those imprisoned inside."[192]

But contrary to popular belief, initially the Jewish ghettos were not compulsory. That came later, once the Jews were already concentrated in their living areas. Renowned historian, Salo Wittmayer Baron, wrote that "Jews had fewer duties and more rights than the great bulk of the population. ...They could move freely from place to place with few exceptions, they could marry whomever they wanted, they had their own courts, and were judged according to their own laws. Even in mixed cases with non-Jews, not the local tribunal but usually a special judge appointed by the king or some high official had competence."[193]

A few pages later, continues Prof. Wittmayer Baron, "...The Jewish community enjoyed full internal autonomy. Complex, isolated, in a sense foreign, it was left more severely alone by the State than most corporations. Thus, the Jewish community of pre-Revolutionary days had more competence over its members than the modern Federal, State, and Municipal governments combined [relevant to 1928, year of publication]. Education, administration of justice between Jew and Jew, taxation for communal and State purposes, health, markets, public order, were all within the jurisdiction of the community-corporation, and in addition, the Jewish community was the fountainhead of social work of a quality generally superior to that outside Jewry.

"...A phase of this corporate existence generally regarded by emancipated Jewry as an unmitigated evil was the Ghetto. But it must not be forgotten that the Ghetto grew up voluntarily as a result of Jewish self-government, and it was only in a later development that public law interfered and made it a legal compulsion for all Jews to live in a secluded district."[194]

Thus, relying on each other for their subsistence, the Jews grew closer, cultivated their own literature, and lived modestly and piously. Once again, we see that when Jews stick together, they are unharmed. And once again, we see that when cohesion and unity are not the Jews' choice in life, circumstances impose it upon them from outside. Albeit coercive, it is always unity that keeps them safe.

And yet, despite the safety provided by unity, and the fact that Jews, as Prof. Grant noted, are "inassimilable," as soon as the door opens and the Jews are allowed outside, they begin to mingle in the very same manner that brought upon them the calamity in Spain—cultural assimilation, and, worse yet, *religious assimilation*. Somehow, we always seem to forget the words of our sages, who repeatedly claim, "When they [Israel] are as one man with one heart, they are as a fortified wall against the forces of evil."[195] Indeed, as we have shown throughout this book, the neglect of unity is what caused the ruin of the Temple and the dispersion of the people from its land, and indeed every calamity that struck the Jews since then.

As the Jewish emancipation progressed and German Jews were allowed into the German Christian society, they gradually became estranged from their spiritual roots. Toward the end of the 18th century, they were so eager to be admitted into the Christian society that they would do virtually anything to be accepted. Thus, according to Professors of Jewish culture and history, Steven J. Zipperstein of Stanford University and Jonathan Frankel of the Hebrew University in Jerusalem, in 1799, only a few years after the start of the Jewish emancipation, David Friedlander, one of the Jewish community's most prominent leaders, went as far as to suggest that Berlin Jews would convert to Christianity en masse.[196]

But even without converting, German Jews were willing to relinquish everything their forefathers had held sacred. "In order to prove the absolute loyalty of the Jews to state and country," write Zipperstein and Frankel later in their book, "[the Jews] were ready to remove from the prayer-books any reference to the age-old hope for a return to the ancient homeland in Palestine and to interpret the dispersion of the Jews across the world not as Exile but as of positive value, as the way for the Jews to carry the message of monotheistic ethics to all of mankind, as a divinely ordained mission. Thus, the Reform movement made it possible to claim that the Jews constituted a strictly religious community divested of all national attributes, that they were Germans (or Poles or Frenchmen, as the case might be) of the 'Mosaic persuasion.' In this way, reformed Judaism became the symbol, as it were, of a readiness to trade in age-old beliefs in exchange for civil equality and social acceptance."[197]

The relinquishing of the Jews' connection to Zion, the land of Israel and the desire for the Creator—the Law of Bestowal—symbolizes more than anything the extent to which German Jews had alienated themselves from their heritage. As we have seen so many times, and as we learn from the teachings of our sages throughout history, once the Jews willingly abandon their role, they are forced back into it by the very nations within which they strive to mingle.

Alas, the German Jews did not know this fact. They were in exile, banished from the quality of bestowal and oblivious to their task. They were ignorant of their mistake that the minute they traded cohesion for acceptance by the general society, they put their future and the future of their children in harm's way. While no one could have predicted the magnitude of the horror that would befall them, the path toward it had been paved, and their conduct continued to shore it up.

From approximately 1780 through 1869, despite several setbacks, gradual advancement of the Jewish emancipation took place. Eventually, "The law of equality was passed by the Parliament of the North German Confederation on July 3, 1869. With the extension of this law to the states united within the German Empire, the struggle of Germany's Jews for emancipation achieved success."[198]

But the price of the success was the complete abandonment of everything that had kept the Jews together. According to Werner Eugen Mosse, Professor Emeritus of European History at the University of East Anglia, "In 1843, the first radical Reform society—rejecting circumcision and calling for the moving of the Jewish Sabbath to Sunday— came into existence to Frankfurt. ...In the next two or three decades, the religious Reform movement would re-structure the religious service in most large communities and develop into the Liberal religious movement which dominated twentieth-century German Jewry.

"...The pressure for social integration into general society led many to abandon practices which they felt set up a barrier against social intercourse (e.g. the dietary laws), while the need to be economically competitive forced many to do business on Saturday, the Jewish Sabbath. In addition, many acculturated Jews found themselves repelled by the traditional Jewish service for aesthetic reasons."[199]

"Another aspect of Reform closely tied to education," continues Prof. Eugen Mosse, "was the new ceremony of confirmation. This ceremony, based on Christian models, was intended to supplement (or more rarely, replace) the traditional *bar mitzvah*. Both girls and boys, on graduating from religious school, were given a public oral examination on the bases of the Jewish religion and were then blessed by the rabbi and formally inducted into Judaism."[200]

Thus, just as it happened in Spain some four centuries earlier, the Reform Jews were in effect becoming "Ashkenazi *conversos.*" According to Donald L. Niewyk, Professor Emeritus of History at SMU, "The vast majority of Jews was passionately committed to the well-being of its sole Fatherland, Germany."[201]

And just as it happened in Spain, when the tide began to turn against the Jews, and anti-Semitism began to rise in the Weimar Republic of Germany, the Jews were blissfully oblivious to the sounding alarms. "Not a few saw anti-Semitism as a positive boon that alone could keep the Jews from gradual amalgamation with the larger society and ultimate disappearance as a distinctive religious group," narrates Prof. Niewyk.[202] Without noticing that letting the nations keep us together instead of doing so ourselves bears unimaginable consequences, Dr. Kurt Fleischer, the leader of the Liberals in the Berlin Jewish Community Assembly, argued in 1929 that "Anti-Semitism is the scourge that God has sent us in order to lead us together and weld us together."[203] This, again, proves right the earlier-cited words of Prof. Cohn-Sherbok: "The paradox of Jewish life is that ... without anti-Semitism, we may be doomed to extinction."[204] Indeed, how tragically right they all are.

As it turned out, Hitler, too, thought that the Creator was using the Nazis to do His work. In *Mein Kampf*, he wrote similar words to the abovementioned statement of Isabella, queen of Spain, about the Lord punishing the Jews through the king: "Eternal Nature inexorably avenges the infringement of her commands. Hence today I believe that I am acting in accordance with the will of the Almighty Creator: by defending myself against the Jew, I am fighting for the work of the Lord."[205]

Since the Creator is the quality of love and bestowal, the Jews' emergence from the ghettos exposed their exile from that quality. Consequently, instead of bringing solidarity and mutual responsibility to their host societies, they were spreading egotism, which is ruinous to any society, and were therefore met with intolerance and repulsion soon after their acceptance. German philosopher and anthropologist, Ludwig Feuerbach, connected Jews with egotism in the following manner: "The Jews have maintained their peculiarity to this day. Their principle, their God, is the most practical principle in the world— namely egoism. And moreover, egoism in the form of religion. Egoism is the God who will not let his servants come to shame. Egoism is essentially monotheistic, for it has only one, only self, as its end."[206]

Indeed, who would welcome such a menace into society? It is precisely that egotism that causes each and every nation within which we live to rethink, and eventually regret and repeal its openness.

The one thing that made Jews unique and powerful in ancient times was their unity, their altruism, and as we have shown, that was the one thing that Abraham and Moses wished to give to the world. At first, the nations welcome us into their midst, subconsciously hoping we will share with them that quality. But upon discovering that we are giving them the opposite, their joy turns to disillusionment and anger. As long as we continue to disappoint the nations, we will continue to receive the same treatment, and the trend is showing that the means by which they'll show their disappointment will grow even harsher.

THE LAND OF
UNLIMITED POSSIBILITIES

Once entrenched as a major force in Germany, Reform Judaism spread to the United States, Hungary and a number of countries in Western Europe. This was a result of the emancipation of the German Jewry.[207] A similar process of dispersion occurred with Conservative Judaism,[208] and the two denominations became the predominant religious forces in United States Jewry by the mid 1800s.

In *Response to Modernity: A History of the Reform Movement in Judaism*, Professor Michael A. Meyer of HUC writes that while Reform Judaism in Germany constantly had to defend itself from both the entrenched Orthodox establishment and from government intervention, these impediments did not exist in the US. "True, individually and collectively, Americans were not entirely free of prejudice," Meyer adds, "but in the United States there was no government control over religion, no conservative established church to set the pattern of religious life."[209]

Thus, Reform and Conservative Judaism found in America a land of unlimited possibilities. The mindset of amalgamation with the host, predominantly Christian society, has finally found fertile soil in which to grow. According to Prof. Meyer, "German Jews could never really feel they were partners in shaping the destiny of the nation with which they so much identified. The United States was different in this regard as well. Like the major European nations it had its own profound sense of mission, but that mission rested upon a destiny not only unfulfilled but not even wholly determined. In America, Reform Jews could feel that their own concept of mission might be woven into a larger still inchoate national purpose."[210]

Indeed, with the obvious exception of Israel, the contribution of Jews to the shaping of a nation has never been more substantial than it has, and still is in the United States. Be it economy, entertainment, education, politics, or any other aspect of American life, the Jews play a major, if not leading role.

Never in all of history have Jews been in a better position to fulfill the role for which they were chosen. They are embedded in every corner of American public life and entrenched in the mediums that determine public discourse and public opinion. Considering the predominance of

American culture worldwide, the Jews can now affect change that will impact the entire world.

Put differently, despite antagonism toward the United States coming from other powerful nations, the global culture—and therefore social standards—is still predominantly American. The dominant films come from America, pop music comes primarily from America, the main news outlets come from America, and the internet is dominated by American companies such as Google, Facebook, Microsoft, and Apple. In a sense, America is to the world what New York is to America—if you make it there, you'll make it anywhere.

American Jews, therefore, bear a greater responsibility for offering what they must than any other Jewry, perhaps excluding that of the state of Israel. If American Jewry unites and projects the values of mutual guarantee, the rest of American society will follow. Today, many Americans understand that the principles on which the American Dream was fashioned no longer hold true. Rampant egotism and an excessive sense of self-entitlement have consumed everything that was good about the freedom to speak your mind, to initiate, to work hard and succeed, and to live by your faith.

There is so much violence, distrust, competition, and exploitation in American society that unless a major shift happens very soon, the society will implode. And if that happens, the Jews, as always, will be held at fault. Arguments about Jewish contribution to science, culture, and economy will be rebuffed, and the Jews will be the obvious wrongdoers in everyone's eyes. Anti-Semitism that has been latent for several generations will roar to the surface, and a repeat of the horrors of Nazi Germany cannot be ruled out.

As we have seen throughout this book, Jews and non-Jews alike are keenly aware that the Jews are essentially a task force, a unit built for a very specific mission. In 1976, the Central Conference of American Rabbis (CCAR) adopted a platform which it titled, "Reform Judaism: A Centenary Perspective." In that platform the conference announced, "We have learned that the survival of the Jewish people is of highest priority and that in carrying out our Jewish responsibilities, we help move humanity toward its messianic fulfillment." [211]

Indeed, currently, the Jewish people are the only nation within which cohesion and subsequent revelation, attainment, and acquisition of the quality of the Creator, the quality of bestowal, are possible. Our "messianic fulfillment," whether the conference delegations were aware of it or not, is for all the nations to obtain the qualities just mentioned and enjoy their benefits. Until we fulfill our role, the world will keep blaming us for every adversity and plight that comes upon it. And the more we avoid our mission, the more harshly they will force us back to it.

Prophet Jonah should be a reminder to every Jew that our vocation is preordained and non-negotiable. We can follow it willingly and reap its benefits, or follow it unwillingly and reap the punishments of the world, as history has proven so many times.

In a very willing spirit, the platform's final section is aptly titled, "Hope: Our Jewish Obligation." In that section, CCAR takes a paramount commitment (emphases are the editor's): "...our people has always refused to despair. The survivors of the Holocaust, being granted life, seized it, nurtured it, and, rising above catastrophe, showed humankind that the human spirit is indomitable. The State of Israel ... demonstrates *what a united people can accomplish in history. The existence of the Jew is an argument against despair; Jewish survival is warrant for human hope.*

"We remain God's witness that *history is not meaningless. We affirm that with God's help people are not powerless to affect their destiny.* We dedicate ourselves, as did the generations of Jews who went before us, to *work and wait for that day when* 'They shall not hurt or destroy in all My holy mountain for *the earth shall be full of the knowledge of the Lord* as the waters cover the sea.'"[212]

Indeed, history, especially Jewish history, is not meaningless. It has an educational purpose: to teach us our role in life and to show us the right way from the wrong way, the blissful path from the painful one. Yet, it is our choice which way we want to go.

In his "Introduction to the Book of Zohar," 20th century Kabbalist, Baal HaSulam, relates specifically to the role of the Jewish people at this time: "Bear in mind that in everything there is internality and externality. In the world in general, Israel, the descendants of Abraham, Isaac and Jacob, are considered the internality of the world [closest to the Creator], and the seventy nations [the rest of the nations] are considered the externality of the world. ...Also, there is internality in every person from Israel—the Israel within— which is the point in the heart [desire for the Creator, for bestowal], and there is externality—the inner Nations of the World [all other desires]...

"When a person from Israel enhances and dignifies one's internality, which is the Israel in that person, over the externality, which are the Nations of the World in him ... by so doing, one makes the children of Israel soar upward in the internality, and externality of the world as well. Then the nations of the world ... recognize and acknowledge the value of the children of Israel.

"And if, God forbid, it is to the contrary, and an individual from Israel enhances and appreciates one's externality, which is the nations of the world in him, more than the inner Israel in him, as it is written (Deuteronomy 28), 'The stranger that is in the midst of thee,' meaning the externality in that person rises and soars, and you yourself, the internality, the Israel in you, plunges down? With these actions, one causes the externality of the world in general—the nations of the world—to soar ever higher and overcome Israel, degrading them to the ground, and the children of Israel, the internality in the world, to plunge deep down.

"Do not be surprised that one person's actions bring elevation or decline to the whole world, for it is an unbending law that the general and the particular are as identical as two peas in a pod. And all that applies in the general, applies in the particular, as well. Moreover, the parts make what is found in the whole, for the general can appear only after the appearance of the parts in it, according to the quantity and quality of the parts. Evidently, the value of an act of a part elevates or declines the entire whole."[213]

Moreover, continues Baal HaSulam, "When one increases one's toil in the internality of the Torah and its secrets [exerts to attain the Creator], to that extent one makes the virtue of the internality of the world—which are Israel—soar high above the externality of the world, which are the Nations of the World. And all the nations will acknowledge and recognize Israel's merit over them, until the realization of the words, 'And the people shall take them, and bring them to their place: and the house of Israel shall possess them in the land of the Lord' (Isaiah 14, 2), and also 'Thus says the Lord God, Behold, I will lift up my hand to the nations, and set up my standard to the peoples: and they shall bring thy sons in their arms, and thy daughters shall be carried on their shoulders' (Isaiah 49:22).

"But if, God forbid, it is to the contrary, and a person from Israel degrades the virtue of the internality of the Torah and its secrets, which deals with the conduct of our souls and their degrees [attainment of the Creator and conveyance of that attainment] ... [the nations] will humiliate and disgrace the children of Israel, and regard Israel as superfluous, as though the world has no need for them."[214]

When that happens, he adds, "the externality of the entire world, being the Nations of the World, intensify and revoke the Children of Israel—the internality of the world. In such a generation, all the destructors among the Nations of the World raise their heads and wish primarily to destroy and to kill the Children of Israel, as it is written (*Yevamot* 63), 'No calamity comes to the world but for Israel.' This means, as it is written in the above corrections, that they cause poverty, ruin, robbery, killing, and destruction in the whole world."[215]

In conclusion, if we carry out our role and pass on the light of benevolence to the world, the quality of the Creator, the internality that Baal HaSulam speaks of, then "the internality of the Nations of the World, the Righteous of the Nations of the World, will overpower and submit their externality, which are the destructors. And the internality of the world, too, which is Israel, shall rise in all their merit and virtue over the externality of the world, which are the nations. Then, all the nations of the world will recognize and acknowledge Israel's merit over them.

"And they shall follow the words (Isaiah 14:2), 'And the people shall take them, and bring them to their place: and the house of Israel shall possess them in the land of the Lord.' And also (Isaiah 49:22), 'And they shall bring thy sons in their arms, and thy daughters shall be carried on their shoulders.'"[216] (Repetition of the quotes is in the original text.)

It may seem like a hefty task for such a small number of people to make such a great difference in the world, but in truth, the success or failure of our efforts depends on one and one thing only—our unity. And so, to remind ourselves of the paramount role that unity plays in our success as a nation and in the success of our mission, the next chapter will be dedicated to the words of our sages throughout the ages as they describe their thoughts about unity. Subsequently, we will examine the means by which we can achieve that unity.

CHAPTER 8

Together Forever

Unity, Unity, and Unity Once Again

As has been said throughout the book, unity has been Israel's "insurance" against all evils, the ultimate panacea. And yet, by now our egotism has so evolved that we can no longer maintain unity unless our very survival depends on it. This fault was noticed by friends and foes alike.

In a paper he published in June 1940, Baal HaSulam noted that our troubles come from lack of unity. He wrote that we are "like a pile of nuts, united into a single body from outside by a sack that wraps and aggregates them."[217] However, he continues, "That measure of unity does not make them a uniform body, and even the slightest movement of the sack inflicts racket and separations among them, by which they come to constant partial unifications and separations. All that is lacking is the natural unification from within, and the power of their unity derives from external situations. Concerning us, it is a very painful matter."[218]

In Chapter 5 we mentioned Baal HaSulam's essay, "There Is a Certain People," in which he writes that Haman relied on the Jews' separation from one another as the key to his triumph over them. Haman knew that separation among them meant that they were also separated from the Creator, the quality of bestowal, the force that creates reality. For this reason, Haman believed he could exploit the weakness of the Jews to do away with them. Much to his regret, Mordechai perceived that danger just as well as Haman, and "went to correct that flaw, as it is explained in the verse, 'the Jews gathered,' etc., 'to gather themselves together, and to stand up for their lives.' That is, they saved themselves by uniting."[219]

A more contemporary "Haman," Adolf Hitler, also noticed the trait of unity in Jews, and noted the lack of it among us today. In *Mein Kampf*, Hitler wrote, "The Jew is only united when a common danger forces him to be or a common booty entices him; if these two grounds are lacking, the qualities of the crassest egoism come into their own, and in the twinkling of an eye the united people turns into a horde of rats, fighting bloodily among themselves."[220]

Therefore, before we go about discussing how we can achieve unity and thus prevent future calamities such as those that our people has experienced throughout the generations, we will dedicate this chapter to excerpts from rabbis and Jewish scholars of all generations. These will remind us of the wall-to-wall agreement concerning the paramount importance of unity and solidarity. Since our essential substance is the will to receive, to succeed in uniting, it is vital that we first come to *want* unity—even if merely as a shield against afflictions—before we go about establishing it. Below are our sages' inspiring words.

UNITY—THE HEART AND SOUL OF ISRAEL

Although Beit Shamai and Beit Hillel were disputed, they treated each other with fondness and friendship, to keep what was said (Zachariah 8), "Love truth and peace."

Babylonian Talmud, *Yevamot*, Chapter 1, p 14b

In Israel is the secret to the unity of the world. This is why they are called "men."

Rav Avraham Yitzhak HaCohen Kook (the Raiah),
Orot HaKodesh [*Lights of Holiness*], Vol. 2, p 415

It was established on Mount Sinai that the children of Israel became one nation. This is why it is written, "I," in singular form, because to the extent of the unity between them, His Godliness is present over the children of Israel.

Yehuda Leib Arie Altar (ADMOR of Gur), *Sefat Emet* [*Truthful Lips*],
VaYikra [Leviticus], *Parashat BaHar* [Portion, On the Mount], *TARLAV* (1893)

It is known that from the perspective of the mind, each person is an individual ... but from the perspective of the heart, there is unity in Israel.

Rabbi Shmuel Bornstein, *Shem MiShmuel*
[*A Name Out of Samuel*], *Shemot* [Exodus], *TAR'AH* (1915)

When Israel entered the land, they were completely one nation. The evidence of that is that as long as Israel did not cross the Jordan and did not arrive at the land, they were not punished ... until they crossed and became responsible for one another.

Thus, Israel did not become responsible for one another because one is called *Arev* [guarantor/responsible for] when one is *Meorav* [mixed/mingled] with another, and Israel did not become connected into being entirely one nation until they arrived at the land and were together in the land, and had one place, the land of Israel. And through the land of Israel, they are completely one nation.

Judah Loewe ben Bezalel (the Maharal of Prague),
Eternal Paths, "Path of Righteousness," Chapter 6

Because the 600,000 souls of Israel are all tied to one another like a woven rope, united as one without separation, should you shake the beginning of the tightened rope, you will shake all of it. Therefore, should one man sin, wrath will be upon the entire congregation. The reason is that all of Israel are responsible for one another.

...One who blemishes, blemishes all the souls of Israel until he returns to mend what he had corrupted in his soul. ...It means that since the parts relate to one another, they will not be separated.

Rabbi Eliyahu Di Vidash, *Beginning of Wisdom*,
"Gate of Fear," Chapter 14

The soul ascends and becomes complete primarily when all the souls mingle and become one, for then they rise toward the sanctity, for sanctity is one. ...Therefore, first, one should take upon oneself the commandment, "Love your neighbor as yourself," as our Rav wrote that it is impossible to utter words of prayer unless by peace, when one connects with all the souls of Israel.

Rabbi Nathan Sternhertz, *Likutey Halachot*
[*Assorted Rules*], "Synagogue Rules," Rule no. 1

Although the bodies of the whole of Israel are divided, their souls are a single unity at the root. ...This is why Israel are commanded to unity of the hearts, as it is written, "And Israel encamped there," in singular form [in Hebrew], which means that they were corresponding below, meaning they had unity.

Rabbi David Solomon Eibenschutz,
Willows of the Brook, Nassoh [Take]

Israel were not given the Torah [Law of Bestowal] before they had acquired complete unity, as we wrote regarding the verse (Exodus 19:2), "And Israel encamped there before the mount." Moses too would not receive at all, as our sages said, (*Berachot* [Blessings], 32a) that the Creator said to Moses concerning the calf, "Come down from your greatness, for I have given you greatness only for Israel."

Rabbi Moshe Alsheich, *Moses' Law*,
concerning *Deuteronomy*, 33:4-5.

When Israel have unity, there is no end to their attainment.

Rabbi Elimelech Weisblum of Lizhensk,
Noam Elimelech [*The Pleasantness of Elimelech*], Pinehas

"Jerusalem that is built as a city that is joined together" (Psalms, 122:3)—a city that makes all of Israel friends.

Jerusalem Talmud, *Hagigah*, Chapter 3, Rule 6

You, the friends who are here, as you were in fondness and love before, henceforth you will not part from one another, until the Lord rejoices with you and declares peace over you. And by your merit there will be peace in the world, as it is written, "For the sake of my brothers and friends I will speak, 'May peace be in you.'"

Rav Yehuda Ashlag (Baal HaSulam),
*The Book of Zohar with the Sulam Commentary,
Aharei Mot* [After the Death], item 66

UNITY—ISRAEL'S SALVATION

The prime defense against calamity is love and unity. When there are love, unity, and friendship between each other in Israel, no calamity can come over them. ...Even if they worship idols, but there is bonding among them, and no separation of hearts, they have peace and quiet, and no Satan or evildoer, and all the curses and suffering are removed by that [unity].

This is the meaning of what is said, "You are standing this day, all of you." It means that although you have heard all the bludgeons of the covenant that are written above, you are standing nonetheless, and you will have revival by your heads, judges, elders, officers, and all the men of Israel being all with one heart and with love... Through bonding you will be able to walk through the bludgeons and they will not reach you or harm you at all.

"That He may establish you today as His people" means that by that you will have revival, you will be saved from all calamities. Afterwards He said to them, "Now not with you alone am I making this covenant," meaning that being saved from any harm by bonding was not promised only to Moses' generation. Rather, "But with those who stand here with us today ... and with those who are not with us here today," meaning that all future generations have been promised it— to pass through all the bludgeons of the covenant, and that they will not be harmed, through the unity and bonding that will be among them.

Rabbi Kalonymus Kalman Halevi Epstein,
Maor VaShemesh [*Light and Sun*], Nitzavim [Standing].

We are commanded at each generation to strengthen the unity among us so our enemies do not rule over us.

Rabbi Eliyahu Ki Tov,
The Book of Consciousness, Chapter 16

The Lord said to David: "When troubles come upon Israel for their iniquities, let them stand before Me in one association and confess their iniquities before Me... When Israel gather before Me and stand before Me in one association, and say before Me a prayer for forgiveness, I will grant them."

Tanna Devei Eliyahu Zuta, Chapter 13

When one includes oneself with all of Israel and unity is made, the Lord is present in the unity. At that time no harm shall come to you.

Rabbi Menahem Nahum of Chernobyl,
Maor Eynaim [*Light of the Eyes*], VaYetzeh [And Jacob Went Out]

When they [Israel] quarrel and there is unity among them nonetheless, then unity is more precious. This is why "Moab was in great fear of the people," for although it is quarrelling, it is still It (singular form), hence the "great fear."

Rabbi Moshe Taitelboim,
Yishmach Moshe [*Let Moses Rejoice*], Balak, p 71b

Therefore, he said, "Gather together and hear, you sons of Jacob," precisely "Gather together," for he revealed to them that the primary element of correction is the advice to gather together, meaning that there will be unity, love, and peace in Israel, that they will gather together to speak to one another of the final purpose. Thus they will be rewarded with completeness of the counsel, for Israel and the Torah [Law of Bestowal] are all one, to the extent of peace and unity in Israel.

Rabbi Nathan Sternhertz,
Likutey Halachot [*Assorted Rules*],
"Rules of the Ninth of Av and Fasts," Rule no. 4

Thus, Israel will be a holy congregation and one association, as one man with one heart. Then, when unity restores Israel as before, Satan will have no place in which to place error and external forces. When they are as one man with one heart, they are as a fortified wall against the forces of evil.

Rabbi Shmuel Bornstein,
Shem MiShmuel [*A Name Out of Samuel*], VaYakhel
[And Moses Assembled], *TAR'AV* (1916)

This is the mutual guarantee on which Moses worked so hard before his death, to unite the children of Israel. All of Israel are each other's guarantors [responsible for one another], meaning that when all are together, they see only good.

Rabbi Simcha Bonim Bonhart of Peshischa,
A Broadcasting Voice, Part 1, Balak

All the souls of Israel are in complete unity and at the same level, like a caravan traveling in the desert among evil beasts with arms and other tactics, but the evil beasts are afraid to approach them. But when they journeyed from the place where they had parked, a man had stayed there alone, and he was promptly put to death by the animals for he had separated from his party.

Rabbi David Solomon Eibenschutz, *Willows of the Brook* (related to *Rosh Hashanah* that occurs on the Sabbath)

The foundation of the wickedness of evil Haman, on which he had built his request of the king to sell the Jews to him ... is what he had begun to argue, "There is a certain people scattered abroad and dispersed," etc. He cast his filth saying that that nation deserves to be destroyed, for separation rules among them, they are all full of strife and quarrel, and their hearts are far from one another. However, He put the healing before the blow [took preventing measures] ... by hastening Israel to unite and adhere to one another, to all be one, as one man, and this is what saved them, as in the verse, "Go, gather together all the Jews."

Rabbi Azarya Figo, *Binah Leltim*
[*Understanding for Occasions*], Part 1, Sermon 1 for Purim

Because they sinned, that force of unity was taken from the wicked and was given to the children of Israel... This is the great mercy we should always remember. Also, we should trust it for because our intention is good, we are certain to succeed, since the force of unity ... assists us.

Yehuda Leib Arie Altar (ADMOR of Gur),

Sefat Emet [*Truthful Lips*], *Beresheet* [Genesis],

Parashat Noah [Portion, Noah], *TARLAV* (1875)

The matter of social unity, which can be the source of every joy and success, applies particularly among bodies and bodily matters in people, and the separation between them is the source of every calamity and misfortune.

Rav Yehuda Ashlag (Baal HaSulam),

The Writings of Baal HaSulam, "The Freedom," p 426

UNITY MEANS REDEMPTION

Elijah comes only to correct the deficiency that was present at the time of his arrival. This is why Elijah comes primarily to settle the dispute, for that certainly unites and ties Israel as one, until they are worthy of redemption from the exile. It is so because Israel are not redeemed from exile before they are completely one, as it is said in the Midrash, that Israel are not redeemed until they are one.

Judah Loewe ben Bezalel (the Maharal of Prague),

Innovations of Legends, Part 4, *Masechet* Matrimony, p 63

It is a wonderful thing that two prophets prophesied a very significant prophecy regarding the time of redemption: "And I will give them one heart" (Jeremiah, 32:39, Ezekiel, 11:19). Indeed, they knew what they were prophesying; the devil of separation-of-the-heart has been lurking for our nation from time immemorial.

Avraham Kariv, *Atarah LeYoshnah* [*Restoring Old Glory*],
"The State and the Spirit," p 251

It is also clear that the immense effort required of us on the rugged road ahead requires unity as strong and as solid as steel, from all factions of the nation without any exceptions. If we do not come out with united ranks toward the mighty forces standing in our way then we are doomed before we even started.

Rav Yehuda Ashlag (Baal HaSulam),
The Writings of Baal HaSulam, "The Nation," p 487

CHAPTER 9

Plurally Speaking

Effecting Social Cohesion

through the

Social Environment

Persecution and anti-Semitism, or its more contemporary term, Judeophobia, have been the lot of our people for (at least) the past two millennia. And yet, as we have seen throughout the book, the hatred of Jews did not spring up out of thin air. It is rooted in the fundamental, though usually unconscious demand of every human being that the Jews must and will usher them into the attainment of life's purpose: to receive boundless delight and pleasure.

Thus far we have discussed the goal and role of the Jewish nation, and the reason for our anguish throughout the ages. Henceforth we will discuss the principles we need to follow in order to achieve our goal, which coincides with the goal of humanity.

THE DRIVE FOR SUPERIORITY

In Chapter 2 we introduced the words of our sages concerning the fundamental desires at the foundation of Creation, and the four levels that make up the desire to receive. Briefly, we said that reality consists of a desire to bestow pleasure and a desire to receive it. We learned from those sages that the desire to receive pleasure is divided into four levels, known as "still," "vegetative," "animate," and "speaking." However, it is still essentially one desire that wears different attire at different levels of development.

For example, the most basic desire in existence is to sustain oneself. At the human level, that desire would appear as being content with a shelter, be it even a tin hut, and the means to keep warm, clothed, and fed. This is the still level of desire. Just like inanimate materials that keep their atoms and molecules together but do very little else, such a person will wish only to sustain oneself, seemingly "keeping one's atoms and molecules together" and very little else.

At the vegetative level of desire, a person will want to sustain oneself on the same level as everyone else. As all plants of a certain kind blossom and wither at the same time, such a person will want to be the same as everyone in one's town or village, or follow the latest trend seen on TV.

If everyone is poor, that person will not feel poor as long as his or her standard of living is on a par with that of the social environment. And if the new trend in clothing is to wear the left shoe on the right foot, and vice-versa, the vegetative-level person will be more comfortable wearing the wrong shoe on the wrong foot, so long as he or she is in line with the prevailing trend in fashion.

The animate-level person differs from the vegetative-level one in that he or she begins to seek self-expression. Such a person no longer settles for being like everyone else, but needs to establish one's individuality. For the most part, this level leads to enhanced creativity and distinction in that person's subject of choice.

The speaking (human) level is the most complex and tricky. Here it is not enough to express oneself. On this level, the desire is to be *superior*. This is the desire that makes people want to be *recognized* as special, even unique. In other words, on that level we constantly *compare* ourselves to others.

Moreover, these days we cannot settle for being the best at something; we strive to be the best *ever*. Think of the sports statistics we constantly hear about: Michael Phelps' ambition to break Mark Spitz's record of seven gold medals in swimming in the 1972 Olympic Games, or basketball players comparing themselves to Michael Jordan, or Roger Federer's drive to keep winning tennis titles, even though he has already won more Grand Slam tournaments than anyone before him. And yet, he is still troubled by the fact that he has not won an Olympic gold medal.[221]

Sports may be a conspicuous example, but it is certainly not the exception; it is rather the norm. The film that earned the most money in its first week, the album that sold the most copies, the company that sells the most phones/computers/cars—competition and comparisons are everywhere. Ask a high school student, "Are you doing well in school?" and you will probably get an answer along the lines of, "I'm on the top five percent of my class" (assuming you have asked a good student). Thus, being good is no longer good enough; *superiority* has become the motto of our lives. We call it "being somebody." Being me is not good enough; if I am not *somebody*, I am nobody.

There is a Hassidic tale about Rabbi Meshulam Zusha of Hanipol (Anipoli), brother of the renowned Rabbi Elimelech of Lizhensk, one of the founders of the Hassidut. Rabbi Zusha used to say, "When I go to heaven, if I am asked, 'Why weren't you Elimelech (Zusha's esteemed brother), I will know what to say. But if I am asked 'Why weren't you Zusha,' I will not know what to say."[222] The moral is clear—be yourself and actualize your potential; this is what you need to do in life.

But Rabbi Zusha lived in the 18th century. Today, such a moral would be unacceptable because what matters is not who you are, but who you are *compared to others*, your position in the class percentage division. When the primary motto in society is so alienating and antisocial, it is no wonder that our society is falling apart.

FROM ME, TO WE, TO ONE

With our current knowledge of human nature, we cannot avoid this competitive and alienating attitude because it is coming from within us, a dictation of the fourth, speaking level of desire, and we cannot stop the evolution of desires, just as we cannot stop the evolution of the whole of Nature. Moreover, if we are to achieve the purpose of creation of becoming similar to the Creator, we will need a robust desire as the fuel thrusting us forward, which means that we must not diminish or oppress our desires, or we will not attain our life's goal.

And yet, not being able to stop the heightening of our self-centered desires does not mean we must yield to a trend of worsening human relations on all levels. Our society does not *have* to decline to a point where all we can do is to stock up on supplies, take cover, and lay low in wait for some miracle to save us from our fellow men and women.

In fact, even if we chose to try to shield ourselves, our nation's mournful history indicates, and the law of Nature dictates that the nations will not permit us to remain passive. When troubles ensue, it is guaranteed that the Jews will be blamed for it once more and consequently tormented, perhaps worse than ever. However, contrary to past ordeals, there is much we can do to prevent this from unfolding.

RECALL THE FIRST "EGO-WARRIOR"

When the speaking level of desires first erupted as egotism, Babylon was at its peak, and Abraham was the one faced with trying to solve the mystery of his people's social decline. His countryfolk were so immersed in building their tower that they completely abandoned their camaraderie. They were no longer "of one language and of one speech" (Genesis 11:1); all they cared about was the tower.

The book, *Pirkey de-Rabbi Eliezer* (*Chapters of Rabbi Eliezer*), portrays Abraham's dismay with his people's new passion: "Rabbi Pinhas says that there were no stones there [in Babylon] to build the city and the tower. What did they do? They fashioned bricks and burned them like artisans until they built it [the tower] seven miles high. Those who would lift up the bricks climbed up from the east, and those who climbed down would descend on the west. And if a man fell and died they would pay him no mind. But if a brick fell, they would sit down and wail saying, 'When will another come up in its stead?' When Abraham, son of Terah, walked by and saw them building the city and the tower, he cursed them in the name of God."[223]

But Abraham did more than curse the builders. First, he tried to mend the rift and bring his people back together. *Midrash Rabah* tells us that Abraham brought together all the people in the world,[224] and Rabbi Behayei Ben Asher tells us how he exposed Nimrod's pretence of supernal powers. In his *Midrash, Rabeinu* [our Rav] *Behayei*, he writes, "[Nimrod] said to him, 'I created the earth and the heaven with my power.' Abraham replied, '...when I came out of the cave, I saw the sun rising in the East and setting in the West. Make it rise in the West and set in the East, and I will bow unto you. But if not, the one who gave my hand the strength to burn the statues will give me strength and I will kill you.' Nimrod said to his counselors, 'What shall be the sentence of this one?' They replied, 'He is the one of whom we said, 'A nation shall come forth from him and inherit this world and the next world.' And now, as the sentence he had decreed, so shall be done unto him. Promptly, they threw him into the furnace. At that time the Lord filled with mercy over him and saved him, as it is written, 'I am the Lord, who brought you out of Ur of the Chaldeans.'"[225]

Following his heated debate with the king, Abraham took his family, his students, and his possessions and fled from Babylon. Along the way he collected into his entourage people who agreed with his message—"When faced with egotism, unite above it." In other words, when hatred breaks out among friends, make the common goal of revealing the Creator—the quality of bestowal, the fundamental force that creates reality—more important than the rivaling parties, and thus unite above the rivalry. The bonuses of such deeds are enhanced unity, subsequent acquisition of the quality of bestowal by the former adversaries, and consequently, the revelation of the Creator.

The above sentence describes the essence of the fusion, the mending of the rift with which Abraham attempted to furnish his countryfolk. And that essence—unity above differences enhances cohesion and (if you want it to) reveals the Creator—has never changed. In fact, it will *never* change, as it is Nature's Law of Bestowal.

As detailed in the Introduction to this book, Abraham's group succeeded in uniting and grew into what became the people of Israel, a nation whose common trait is the desire for the Creator. Through unity above differences, as explained in Chapter 1, Israel developed a method by which to shift one's thinking from the "me" mode to the "we" mode, thus perceiving the "One," the Creator.

Thus, while Israel was going from strength to strength by employing unity over egotism, the rest of the world was experiencing episodes of ebb and flow, with empires rising and falling and the hedonistic culture of self-indulgence assuming predominance. For this reason, even today, in the most hedonistic of all eras, Abraham's monotheism is the predominant notion of deity, while the Tower of Babylon is a symbol of human conceit and folly.

This is why the only ones who can educate the world as to the way one can grow as wise as Abraham are those who were his students, the children of Israel, known worldwide as Jews. This wisdom was Abraham's legacy to them, and passing it on as he did is their obligation to the world.

THE WARRIOR'S LEGACY
LEFT FOR HIS PROGENY

Today, enough people understand that the only way to avert a global catastrophe is to unite. It may be called by other terms, such as "collaboration," "coordination," or "consideration," but whatever the term, it is fair to say that we already understand that we are interdependent and interconnected. This reality creates a situation where we are *de facto* united in all our global systems. However, to the extent that we are connected, we are also emotionally alienated and resentful about the situation.

One way to resolve this contrast is to try to "de-globalize" ourselves. While there is no doubt that breaking down the supply chain from developing countries and producing everything inland would cause massive economic and financial challenges, some may say it is worth the price. Perhaps, but worth it or not, no one denies that isolationism will have a hefty price tag. Moreover, in the eyes of some, this notion is completely unrealistic. Economist Mark Vitner, for one, described attempting to untie the global interconnectedness as "trying to unscramble scrambled eggs. It just can't be done that easily."[226]

The contrary option to de-globalization is to embrace globalization, expand it, coordinate it, perfect it, and at the same time learn to like each other so that *everyone* benefits from the prosperity. All we need in order to achieve it is the method by which we shift our thought patterns from me (focusing on myself), to we (focusing on all the people), to one (focusing on society as a single entity).

Today, nearly 4,000 years after Abraham's escape from Babylon, the world is ready to listen. We have all suffered enough, and we have all grown too smart to think that we can make it on our own, that we can show Mother Nature, or God, that we don't need her because we are stronger and wiser.

WHY FORM A SOCIETY THAT TOUTS COHESION?

In Chapter 1, we discussed the concept of "equivalence of form" saying that if you are similar to something, you can see it, identify it, reveal it. It will be easier for us to understand that concept if we consider how radio receivers work. A receiver can pick up waves only when it creates identical waves within it. Similarly, we detect things that seemingly exist on the outside—but only according to what we have created within. This is how we discover the Creator, the quality of bestowal, by forming that quality within us, thus also discovering it outside of us.

It is this principle, "equivalence of form," that made Abraham's method so successful. His group created that quality among themselves and thus discovered the Creator. That is, by moving from the "me" mode to the "we" mode, they discovered the "one" mode, the Creator, the only mode that really does exist.

In today's world, the obtaining of social cohesion is of paramount importance to our survival. We might consider the revelation of the Creator an "accessory" of sorts, were it not for the fact that the Creator is the quality of bestowal, a trait without which we will never achieve unity, and hence never mend the global rift that is threatening to wrench the world into a global confrontation. This is why it is vital that we expedite the spreading of Abraham's method for achieving unity through equivalence of form.

To do that, we must first abandon a common belief in our society—the idea that we have "free choice." Science shows that there is no such thing, at least not in the way we normally think of it—that we do what we want by our own free choice. In recent years, data that proves our dependence on society has been piling up. These studies show that not only our sustenance depends on society, but even our thoughts, aspirations, and chances of success in life. In fact, even the very definition of success is subject to the whims of society. And last but not least, to a great extent, our physical health is significantly affected by society.

On September 10, 2009, *The New York Times* published a story titled, "Are Your Friends Making You Fat?" by Clive Thompson.[227] In his story, Thompson describes a fascinating experiment performed in Framingham, Massachusetts. In the experiment—which was later published in the celebrated book, *Connected: The Surprising Power of Our Social Networks and How They Shape Our Lives—How Your Friends' Friends' Friends Affect Everything You Feel, Think, and Do*—the lives of 15,000 people were documented and registered periodically over fifty years. Professors Nicholas Christakis' and James Fowler's analysis of the data revealed astonishing discoveries about how we affect one another on all levels—physical, emotional, and mental—and how ideas can be as contagious as viruses.

Christakis and Fowler had found that there was a network of interrelations among more than 5,000 of the participants. They discovered that in the network, people mutually affected one another. "By analyzing the Framingham data," Thompson wrote, "Christakis and

Fowler say they have for the first time found some solid basis for a potentially powerful theory in epidemiology: that good behaviors—like quitting smoking or staying slender or being happy—pass from friend to friend almost as if they were contagious viruses. The Framingham participants, the data suggested, influenced one another's health just by socializing. And the same was true of bad behaviors— clusters of friends appeared to 'infect' each other with obesity, unhappiness, and smoking. Staying healthy isn't just a matter of your genes and your diet, it seems. Good health is also a product, in part, of your sheer proximity to other healthy people."[228]

Even more surprising was the researchers' discovery that these infections could "jump" across connections. They discovered that people could affect each other even if they did not know each other! Moreover, Christakis and Fowler found evidence of these effects even three degrees apart (friend of a friend of a friend). In Thompson's words, "When a Framingham resident became obese, his or her friends were 57 percent more likely to become obese, too. Even more astonishing… it appeared to skip links. A Framingham resident was roughly 20 percent more likely to become obese if the friend of a friend became obese— even if the connecting friend didn't put on a single pound. Indeed, a person's risk of obesity went up about 10 percent even if a friend of a friend of a friend gained weight."[229]

Quoting Professor Christakis, Thompson wrote, "In some sense we can begin to understand human emotions like happiness the way we might study the stampeding of buffalo. You don't ask an individual buffalo, 'Why are you running to the left?' The answer is that the whole herd is running to the left."[230]

But there is more to social contagion than watching one's weight or heart condition. In a lecture on TED, Professor Christakis explained that our social lives, and hence— judging by the previous paragraphs—much of our physical lives, depend on the quality and strength of our social networks and what runs through the veins of that network. In his words, "We form social networks because the benefits of a connected life outweigh the costs. If I were always violent toward you ... or made you sad ... you would cut the ties to me and the network would disintegrate. So the spread of good and valuable things is required to sustain and nourish social networks. Similarly, social networks are required for the spread of good and valuable things like love, and kindness, and happiness, and altruism, and ideas. ...I think social networks are fundamentally related to goodness, and what I think the world needs now is more connections."[231]

But we are not only affected by the people around us. We are significantly affected by the media, by politics, both national and international, and we are affected by the economy. In *Runaway World: How Globalization Is Reshaping Our Lives*, renowned sociologist Anthony Giddens succinctly, yet accurately, expresses our concurrent connectedness and bewilderment: "For better or worse, we are being propelled into a global order that no one fully understands, but which is making its effects felt upon all of us."[232]

In recent years, the corporate world has picked up on the notion, and trainings and courses galore have surfaced on the internet, offering to leverage from the new trend: social contagion. In *Homo Imitans: The Art of Social Infection: Viral Change in Action*, psychiatrist and business leadership consultant, Dr. Leandro Herrero, offers a witty summary of human nature in regard to the influence of the social environment: "We are intellectually complex, rationally stylish, highly enlightened, unsophisticated copying machines."[233] And to complete his irony on the merits of human nature, he writes, "The threads of the rich tapestry of behaviors of Homo Sapiens are made of imitation and influence."[234]

However, the problem is not with our behavior toward each other or toward Earth, not that there is much to pride ourselves on regarding our treatment of each other and of Mother Earth. And yet, our behavior is a symptom of a deeper change, an outburst of egotism at the speaking level of desire, to which no one has a solution.

That said, many people already understand that the change must come from within us. Pascal Lamy, Director-General of the World Trade Organization (WTO), stated that "The real challenge today is to change our way of thinking—not just our systems, institutions or policies. We need the imagination to grasp the immense promise—and challenge—of the interconnected world we have created. ...The future lies with more globalization, not less, more cooperation, more interaction between peoples and cultures, and even greater sharing of responsibilities and interests. It is unity in our global diversity that we need today."[235]

Indeed, Lamy is right in many respects. In recent years, neuroscientists have been abuzz over a relatively new discovery, mirror-neurons. In brief, mirror-neurons are cells located in a region between the prefrontal and motor cortices of the brain, and are involved in preparing and executing limb movements. However, according to a story published in *Psychology Today*, they also play a vital role in our social interconnection. "In 2000, Vilayanur Ramachandran, the charismatic neuroscientist, made a bold prediction: 'mirror neurons will do for psychology what DNA did for biology.' ...For many, they have come to represent all that makes us human.

"For his 2011 book, *The Tell-Tale Brain*, Ramachandran took his claims further. ...he argues that mirror neurons underlie empathy, allow us to imitate other people, that they accelerated the evolution of the brain, that they help explain the origin of language, and most impressively of all, that they prompted the great leap forward in human culture that happened about 60,000 years ago. 'We could say mirror neurons served the same role in early hominin evolution as the Internet, Wikipedia, and blogging do today,' he concludes.

"Ramachandran is not alone. Writing for *The Times* (London) in 2009 about our interest in the lives of celebrities, the eminent philosopher, A.C. Grayling, traced it all back to those mirror neurons. 'We have a great gift for empathy,' he wrote. 'This is a biologically evolved capacity, as shown by the function of 'mirror neurons'.' In the same newspaper this year, Eva Simpson wrote on why people were so moved when Tennis champ Andy Murray broke down in tears. ...'Blame mirror neurons, brain cells that make us react in the same way as someone we're watching.' In a *New York Times* article in 2007, about one man's heroic actions to save another, those cells featured again: 'people have 'mirror neurons,'' Cara Buckley wrote, 'which make them feel what someone else is experiencing.'"[236]

According to Jarrett, it seems that "mirror neurons play a *causal* (emphasis in the source) role in allowing us to understand the goals behind other people's actions. By representing other people's actions in the movement-pathways of our own brain, so the reasoning goes, these cells provide us with an instant simulation of their intentions—a highly effective foundation for empathy."[237]

While there are quite a few dissenters to the theories surrounding mirror-neurons, it is clear that our bodies dedicate portions of the brain explicitly for communication with others. In that manner, we *physically* connect with others *without* having physical contact with them, but only eye contact. In a sense, these cells validate the words of Christakis and Fowler, "The great project of the twenty-first century—understanding how the whole of humanity comes to be greater than the sum of its parts—is just beginning. Like an awakening child, the human superorganism is becoming self-aware, and this will surely help us achieve our goals."[238]

COHESION ON A GLOBAL SCALE

Returning for a moment to our common monotheistic forefather, after the expulsion from Babylon, Abraham established an isolated society that moved as a group and functioned in mutual guarantee. He created a social environment that supported bonding, unity, and cohesion, and attached all those elements to the acquisition of the quality of bestowal, the Creator. Our task today is to do just that, but on a global scale.

Because we really have become aware that we are a superorganism, clearly, we must function as one—in reciprocity and mutual responsibility toward each other. But since we cannot teach the entire world how to function in this manner, we need to *show* the world an example, and the world will do the rest through our ability to empathize, or as Dr Herrero put it, by "imitation and influence." After all, when people see a good idea they naturally embrace it.

Therefore, when people see that the Jews have something that could work well for them, and that the Jews desire to share it, they will not only support us, but *join* us. This, as mentioned in the Introduction, is how Abraham gathered more and more people into his company as he was traveling from Babylon to Canaan, as "thousands and tens of thousands assembled around him, and they are the people of 'the house of Abraham.'"[239]

FOUR FACTORS OF INFLUENCE

In his essay, "The Freedom,"[240] Baal HaSulam discusses extensively the structure of the human psyche, and what we need to focus on in order to achieve a lasting change in our societies. Through a long analysis of the interplay between heredity and the environment, Ashlag explains that four factors combine to make us who we are:

1. Genes;
2. The way our genes manifest through life;
3. The direct environment, such as family and friends;
4. The indirect environment, such as the media, the economy, or friends of friends.

Since we do not choose our parents, we cannot control our gene pool. But our genes are merely the "potential we," not the "actual we" that eventually manifest when we are grownups. The actual "we" consists of all four factors. Moreover, the latter two—which relate to the environment— affect and *change* our genes to suit the environment.

Let's examine the following wonderful example of how the environment changes the genes, as reported by Swanne Gordon of the University of California in an essay titled,

"Evolution Can Occur in Less Than Ten Years," published in *Science Daily*. "Gordon and her colleagues studied guppies— small fresh-water fish... They introduced the guppies into the nearby Damier River, in a section above a barrier waterfall that excluded all predators. The guppies and their descendents also colonized the lower portion of the stream, below the barrier waterfall, that contained natural predators. Eight years later..., the researchers found that the guppies in the low-predation environment... had adapted to their new environment by producing larger and fewer offspring with each reproductive cycle. No such adaptation was seen in the guppies that colonized the high-predation environment... 'High-predation females invest more resources into current reproduction because a high rate of mortality, driven by predators, means these females may not get another chance to reproduce,' explained Gordon. 'Low-predation females, on the other hand, produce larger embryos because the larger babies are more competitive in the resource-limited environments typical of low-predation sites. Moreover, low-predation females produce fewer embryos not only because they have larger embryos but also because they invest fewer resources in current reproduction.'"[241]

Dr. Lars Olov Bygren, a preventive health specialist, documented an even more surprising example of how genes change through environmental effects. John Cloud of *Time Magazine* described Dr. Bygren's research on the long-term effects that extreme feast and famine years had on the residents of the isolated Swedish village of Norrbotten. However, Dr. Bygren observed not only the effects the dietary oscillations had on the people who endured them. He also examined "whether that effect could start even *before* [emphasis added] pregnancy: Could parents' experiences early in their lives somehow change the traits they passed to their offspring?"[242] "It was a heretical idea," writes Mr. Cloud. "After all, we have had a long-standing deal with biology: whatever choices we make during our lives might ruin our short-term memory or make us fat or hasten death, but they won't change our genes—our actual DNA. Which meant that when we had kids of our own, the genetic slate would be wiped clean.

"What's more, any such effects of nurture (environment) on a species' nature (genes) were not supposed to happen so quickly. Charles Darwin, whose *On the Origin of Species...* taught us that evolutionary changes take place over many generations and through millions of years of natural selection. But Bygren and other scientists have now amassed historical evidence suggesting that powerful environmental conditions ... can somehow leave an imprint on the genetic material in eggs and sperm. These genetic imprints can short-circuit evolution and pass along new traits in a single generation."[243]

Baal HaSulam, returning to his essay, "The Freedom," suggested a very similar concept that aligns with Dr. Bygren's findings. In the section, "The Environment as a Factor," he writes (emphases added), "It is true that the desire has no freedom. Rather, it is operated by the above four factors [Genes; how they manifest, direct environment, indirect environment]. And one is *compelled* to think and examine as they suggest, *denied of any strength to criticize or change...*"[244]

In the subsequent section, "The Necessity to Choose a Good Environment," Baal HaSulam adds, "As we have seen, it is a simple thing, and should be observed by each and every one of us. For although everyone has one's own source, the forces are revealed openly only through the environment one is in."[245]

This may sound deterministic because if we are completely governed by our environments, it would seem we have no freedom of choice. And yet, writes Baal HaSulam, we can and *must* choose our environment very carefully. In his words, "There is freedom for the will to initially choose such an environment ... that imparts to one good concepts. If one does not do that, but is willing to enter any environment that one comes by..., one is bound to fall into a bad environment... In consequence, one will be forced into foul concepts..." Such a person, he concludes, "will certainly be punished, not because of one's evil thoughts or deeds, in which one has no choice, but because of not choosing to be in a good environment, for in that there is definitely a choice. Therefore, one who strives to continually choose a better environment is worthy of praise and reward. But here, too, it is not because of one's good thoughts and deeds, ...but because of one's efforts to acquire a good environment, which brings ... good thoughts."[246]

We therefore see that we are all potentially demonic, just as we are potentially angelic. The choice of whether we act out one extreme or the other, or any mixture of the two, depends not on whether we choose to be one way or the other, but on the social environment in which we put ourselves, or that we fashion for ourselves.

As parents, we instinctively warn their children to stay away from the bad kids in the neighborhood, and from the bad students at school. Thus, the awareness of the influence of the environment is inherent in our parental genes, so to speak. Now we must expand that awareness and realize that it is not enough to see that our kids go with "the right" kids. We must start *designing* a new paradigm of thinking for ourselves, as well as for our children. It is a paradigm in which mutual responsibility plays a leading role, mutual care, and camaraderie take the limelight, and public discourse changes accordingly.

In other words, Rabbi Akiva's known maxim, "Love your neighbor as yourself," must take shape and be molded into a way of life for society. That social paradigm is the DNA of our people, our legacy to the world, and what the world, even subconsciously, expects us to pass on.

In an era of consecutive and overlapping global crises, the world is in desperate need of a lifeline, a sliver of hope. We Jews are the only ones who can offer that hope, which is called "mutual guarantee." The next chapter will outline the basics of implementing mutual guarantee as the predominant social paradigm.

CHAPTER 10

Living in an Integrated World

An Integrated World

Requires Integral Education

In the previous chapter, we quoted Baal HaSulam's words from his essay, "The Freedom," stating that we are "compelled to think and examine as they [social environment] suggest," and we are "denied of any strength to criticize or change."[247] Baal HaSulam concluded that to avoid a predetermined fate, we can change the environment, which will in turn change us and our fates. In his words, "One who strives to continually choose a better environment is worthy of praise and reward ... not because of one's good thoughts and deeds ...but because of one's efforts to acquire a good environment, which brings ... good thoughts."[248]

To put it in more contemporary terms, in order to channel our lives and the lives of our children in a positive direction, we need to foster social values that promote the positive direction we wish to instill. We need to educate ourselves, our children, and society at large toward mutual guarantee, mutual responsibility, and eventually toward unity and cohesion. As has been demonstrated throughout the book, it is our vocation as Jews.

We need not conceive any new means of education to achieve this goal. All we need is to shift the means we already use—mass media, the internet, the education system, and our social and familial ties—toward promoting kinship and mutual responsibility, instead of the prevailing narrative of separation and alienation.

Although more often than not, the traits of unity and kinship—and most of all, of mutual responsibility—are dormant within us Jews, it is our duty, indeed our *vocation* to awaken them and offer them as our gift to the world. As has been shown repeatedly in this book, unity is the gift of the Jews, the quality that makes us unique, and the quality we must bestow upon the rest of the world. It is this quality that the world needs today, and it is we who are obliged to nurture it within, and then hand it over to the world.

There are two ways to convey mutual guarantee and the quality of bestowal. The first, intended for those with "points in the heart," as mentioned earlier in the book, is a straightforward study of Kabbalah. According to one's level of interest, it can be done at varying levels of intensity, from watching TV shows to studying intently (and intensely) with a group and a teacher. The other way is a method of unity-oriented education intended to induce cohesion and a sense of mutual responsibility within the society. I will elaborate on these ways one at a time.

THE "POINT-IN-THE-HEART" WAY

For some of us, the way to come by unity is relatively simple. We have already mentioned the "point in the heart," that thirst to understand what life is about, what makes the world go around, the yearning that enabled Adam, Abraham, Isaac, Jacob, Moses, and the entire nation that arose out of the pariahs from Babylon to develop a correction method that turns the evil inclination into goodness. Those who have that point can start studying the texts that Kabbalists have left for us as a means to attain the Creator, the quality of bestowal. Along the way they will learn how to unite on a profound level and will be ready to pass that unity on to others.

In our generation, the most instrumental texts for achieving those purposes are Baal HaSulam's *The Book of Zohar* with the *Sulam* (Ladder) commentary, the writings of the ARI, preferably with Baal HaSulam's commentaries, published in his *Talmud Esser HaSephirot* (*The Study of the Ten Sephirot*), as well as Baal HaSulam's other writings, published in *The Writings of Baal HaSulam*. To make these, and other texts more accessible, we have established a free online library of authentic Kabbalistic texts, translated into dozens of languages.

In the original Hebrew, they can be found at www.kab. co.il, and translations of much of the texts—including even a version of *The Book of Zohar*, titled, *Zohar for All*, which consolidates the text of Rabbi Shimon Bar Yochai (Rashbi) with the commentary of Baal HaSulam—exist in English as well at www.kabbalah.info, for no cost or preconditions whatsoever.

Also available at the above-mentioned web addresses are the writings of my teacher, Rav Baruch Shalom Ashlag (the Rabash), Baal HaSulam's firstborn son, and successor. Although fewer of his writings have been translated into English, all of his essays that teach students how to promote unity in student groups have been published in English in the book, *The Social Writings of Rabash*. For those who prefer hard copies of the texts, all of the above publications exist in print, and can be purchased at www.kabbalahbooks. info or on amazon.com and other online outlets.

Additionally, veteran students have established an Education Center that teaches the basics of Kabbalah and how to implement it so it becomes part of one's daily life, complementing one's personal growth toward obtaining one's goals in life. For more advanced students, I teach a daily three-hour lesson broadcast live on www.kab.tv, with simultaneous interpretations into all major languages—English, Spanish, French, Russian, German, and others. In these lessons, I strive to advance students as quickly and as easily as possible while adhering to the modes of teaching I received from my venerated teacher, the Rabash.

In the last couple of years, we have also been airing shows on US TV channels such as JLTV and Shalom TV, primarily on weekends. Naturally, these shows are not "hardcore" Kabbalah studies, but they are certainly a great reference for anyone who wishes to "wet one's feet" and see what this study is all about.

INTEGRAL, UNITY-ORIENTED EDUCATION

Studying Kabbalah is a wonderful way for achieving unity. It is a method built for precisely that purpose. However, most people do not have a vigorous "point in the heart" that demands answers. It is therefore unlikely that most people will wish to engage in these studies. And yet, the need to establish a cohesive society is a global need, not a personal, Jewish, or even a country-related need.

Dave Sherman, a leading business strategist and sustainability expert, eloquently described the current global predicament in the film, *Crossroads: Labor Pains of a New Worldview*: "The latest Global Risks Report, published by the World Economic Forum, presents an astonishing risks interconnection-map. It clearly reveals how all global risks are interrelated and interwoven, so that economic, ecological, geopolitical, social, and technological risks are hugely interdependent. A crisis in one area will quickly lead to a crisis in other areas. The interconnection and complexity in this map compared to our surprise at the impact and speed of the recent financial crises illustrate the discord that exists between all the systems we have built, and shows just how disconnected we've become. Our attempts at managing these systems are fragmented and simplistic, and not up to the challenges that we face today."[249]

To address precisely that contrast between our own disconnect and the interconnectedness of the systems we have built, we need to develop interconnected thinking, an inclusive perception of our world. Integral Education (IE), the previously mentioned "unity-oriented education," addresses precisely those points.

The term, "integral," according to Thomas J. Murray of the School of Education at the University of Massachusetts, "means many things to many people, and the same is true for Integral Education."[250] The more common perception of IE, as described in Wikipedia, is that it is "the philosophy and practice of education for the whole child: body, emotions, mind, soul, and spirit."[251]

Relating to the whole child in the education process is certainly commendable. However, in today's interconnected world, it is simply not enough. As we have shown in the previous chapter, we learn primarily, if not *only* through the environment. Therefore, the focus of education must be on fashioning an environment that instills our chosen values and information in children and adults alike.

ADULT SCHOOL: A GUIDE FOR THE PERPLEXED

Besides the speaking, human level of Nature, all the other levels—still, vegetative, and animate—operate in mutual guarantee. Homeostasis, as defined in *Webster's Dictionary*, perfectly matches the description of mutual guarantee on the levels below that of the speaking: "A relatively stable state of equilibrium or a tendency toward such a state between the different but interdependent elements or groups of elements of an organism, population, or group."[252]

Our current, predominantly capitalistic society shuns equilibrium, mocks the tendency toward it, and dreads interdependence. In fact, we endorse and campaign for the opposite. We praise individual achievements in sports, business, politics, and the academia, and we idolize those at the top. We overlook those who contribute to the well-being of the collective and cherish individualism and independence.

But a society that functions in this manner cannot last very long. Think of our human bodies. If our bodies conducted themselves by the values that dominate our society, we would not make it past the initial cell-differentiation in the embryonic stage. As soon as cells would begin to form different organs, they would start fighting each other for resources and the embryo would disintegrate. Life would not be possible if any part of it embraced the individualistic values just described. It is *because* life, meaning Nature, adheres to the rules of homeostasis that we can develop and sustain ourselves, and have evolved to the point where we can ponder the nature and purpose of our existence.

Indeed, not only organisms, but our entire planetary ecosystem, even the cosmos, are in a state of homeostasis. When the balance breaks down, troubles soon ensue. An eye-opening and rather amusing report submitted to the U.S. Department of Education in October, 2003 by Irene Sanders and Judith McCabe clearly demonstrates what happens when we tilt an ecosystem off its homeostatic state. "In 1991, an orca—a killer whale—was seen eating a sea otter. Orcas and otters usually coexist peacefully. So, what happened? Ecologists found that ocean perch and herring were also declining. Orcas don't eat those fish, but seals and sea lions do. And seals and sea lions are what orcas usually eat, and their population had also declined. So deprived of their seals and sea lions, orcas started turning to the playful sea otters for dinner.

"So otters have vanished because the fish, which they never ate in the first place, have vanished. Now, the ripple spreads. Otters are no longer there to eat sea urchins, so the sea urchin population has exploded. But sea urchins live off seafloor kelp forests, so they're killing off the kelp. Kelp has been home to fish that feed seagulls and eagles. Like orcas, seagulls can find other food, but bald eagles can't and they're in trouble.

"All this began with the decline of ocean perch and herring. Why? Well, Japanese whalers have been killing off the variety of whales that eat the same microscopic organisms that feed pollock [a type of carnivorous fish]. With more fish to eat, pollock flourish. They in turn attack the perch and herring that were food for the seals and sea lions. With the decline in the population of sea lions and seals, the orcas must turn to otters."[253]

Think of the way we behave toward each other. We are competitive, alienated, isolated from each other, and aspire to excel over others. Keep in mind that this is not the exception, but the *norm*, the values we *all* teach our children as the "right" way to be. This is why an adult school, a guide for the perplexed adult, is necessary.

The way in which this school will operate should vary from place to place and from country to country. Each nation and country has its own mentality and culture, a different level of technological advancement and means of communication, and traditions by which people learn. For this reason, each country, sometimes each city will have to develop its own method of instruction. However, *the fundamental content, the principles that all these adult education systems will teach must be the same.* Otherwise the result will be disparity in the population's commitment to mutual responsibility and the understanding of its importance to our lives.

Let's examine some of the fundamental principles that education toward mutual guarantee should instill.

Prosocial Media

In *The Writings of Baal HaSulam*, Ashlag asserts, "The greatest of all imaginable pleasures is to be favored by people. It is worthwhile to spend all of one's energy and corporeal pleasures to obtain a certain amount of that delightful thing. This is the magnet that has lured the greatest in all the generations, and for which they trivialized the life of the flesh."[254]

Therefore, to alter our social behavior, we must change our *social environment* from one that promotes individuality to one that promotes mutuality. Practically speaking, we can use the media to show how group work yields better results than individual work, and how competition is detrimental to one's happiness and health. Once we realize that there is a greater reward in cooperative conduct than in individualism, it will be easy to collaborate and to share.

In their insightful book, *The Wisdom of Teams: Creating the High-Performance Organization*, authors Jon R. Katzenbach and Douglas K. Smith describe a success story that is worth mentioning in the context of the advantages of teamwork. Burlington Northern Railroad was a successful freight company, and is currently part of a big corporation owned by Berkshire Hathaway, which is controlled by investor Warren Buffett. In 1981, Burlington Northern Railroad was revolutionized by seven men—Bill Greenwood, Mark Cane, Emmett Brady, Ken Hoepner, Dave Burns, Bill Dewitt, and Bill Berry—who used the U.S. deregulation of the railroad industry to speed up the delivery of freight and minimize the cost of delivery. This is how Katzenbach and Smith describe the spirit with which they carried out that revolution: "All real teams share a commitment to their common purpose. But only exceptional team members ... also become deeply dedicated to each other. The seven men developed a concern and commitment for one another as deep as their dedication to the vision they were trying to accomplish. They looked out for each other's welfare, supported each other whenever and however needed, and constantly worked with each other to get done whatever had to get done."[255]

Such a story could be a powerful advocate for the case in favor of unity over competition. The only problem is that in our ultra-competitive world, even unity is used to gain *personal* leverage for the group that is practicing it (or should we say, perpetrating it, due to its misuse). In today's interconnected and interdependent world, this kind of unity is unsustainable.

In our self-centered society, unity will last just as long as it is lucrative for the individuals involved. In the previous chapter, in the section, "From Me, to We, to One," we described the ill effects of competition. At the same time, we acknowledged that "with our current knowledge of human nature, we cannot avoid this competitive and alienating attitude because it is coming from within us, a dictation of the fourth, speaking level of desire, and we cannot stop the evolution of desires."

However, we have already said that we need not impede our evolution, only shift it toward a constructive direction for all. The most instrumental means to achieve this is through mass media. If we develop prosocial media content and bombard ourselves with it as much as we currently bombard ourselves with commercials and infomercials that aim to deplete our bank accounts, we will find ourselves living in a very different society than our current one.

People's contemporary domestic environments contain a great deal of media entertainment, either through the TV or via the internet. A publication by the U.S. Department of Education titled, "Media Guide—Helping Your Child

Through Early Adolescence," stated, "It's hard to understand the world of early adolescents without considering the huge impact of the mass media on their lives. It competes with families, friends, schools, and communities in its ability to shape young teens' interests, attitudes, and values."[256] Regrettably, the majority of interests that the media shapes is antisocial.

For example, an online publication by the University of Michigan Health System states that "Literally thousands of studies since the 1950s have asked whether there is a link between exposure to media violence and violent behavior. All but 18 have answered, 'Yes.' ...According to the AAP (American Academy of Pediatrics), 'Extensive research evidence indicates that media violence can contribute to aggressive behavior, desensitization to violence, nightmares, and fear of being harmed.'"[257]

To understand how much violence young minds absorb, consider this piece of information from the above publication: "An average American child will see 200,000 violent acts and 16,000 murders on TV by age 18."[258] If this number does not seem alarming, consider that there are 6,570 days in eighteen years. This means that on average, by age eighteen a child will have been exposed to slightly more than thirty acts of violence on TV, 2.4 of which are murders, *every single day of his or her young life.*

On the same note, in their book, *Development Through Life: A Psychosocial Approach*, published in 2008, Barbara M. Newman, PhD, and Philip R. Newman describe how "Exposure to many hours of televised violence increases young children's repertoire of violent behavior and increases the prevalence of angry feelings, thoughts, and actions. These children are caught up in the violent fantasy, taking part in the televised situation while they watch."[259] If we remember the mirror-neurons, and consider how much we, and especially children, learn by imitation, we can only imagine what irreversible harm watching violence causes them, and we are already feeling the effects of this ill-education.

Therefore, developing media that is prosocial and pro-mutual responsibility is imperative to our survival as a livable society. It must play a key role in shifting the public atmosphere from alienation to camaraderie. The media provides us with almost everything we know about our world. Even the information we receive from friends and from family usually arrives via the media—the modern version of the grapevine.

But the media does not simply provide us with information. It also offers us tidbits about people we approve or disapprove of, and we form our views based on what we see, hear, or read in the media. Because its power over the public is unrivaled, if the media shifts toward togetherness and unity, it will also shift the worldview of most people toward these values.

Currently, the media focuses on successful individuals, media moguls, mega pop stars, and ultra-successful individuals who made billions on the backs of their competitors. In times of crises, such as after Hurricane Sandy, or during floods, people unite in order to help one another. At such times these stories, which the media airs abundantly, help raise our morale and give us hope that the human spirit is not all bad. Alas, as soon as the next news item comes along, the media chases after that story and disappears, taking with it the belief in the human spirit.

Instead, sensations of suspicion and alienation repossess prime time.

To install a lasting and fundamental change in our worldview, to make us desire the quality of bestowal, the media should present the full picture of reality, and inform us of its interconnected and interdependent structure. To this end, it should produce programs that demonstrate how that quality affects all levels of Nature—inanimate, vegetative, animate, and speaking—and encourage people to emulate it in order to equalize our society with Nature's traits of giving, mutuality, and homeostasis. Instead of talk shows that idolize people who succeeded, these shows should praise people who helped *others* succeed.

If the media shows people caring for each other and puts them on a pedestal primarily because their deeds coincide with the law of Nature, the Law of Bestowal, it will gradually shift the public's favor from self-centeredness to camaraderie. People will begin to feel that there is *personal* gain in being unselfish, possibly much more than the gain there is in selfishness, if there is any gain in it at all.

Today, the predominant message that the media should portray is, "Unity is fun, and it's also good for you; join in!" There are ample ways the media can show us that unity is a gift.

Although every scientist knows that no system in Nature operates in isolation, and that interdependence is the name of the game, most of us are unaware of it. When we see how every physical organ works to benefit the whole body, how bees collaborate in hives, how a school of fish swims in such unison that it can be mistaken for a single giant fish, and how chimpanzees help other chimps, or even humans, without any reward in return, we will *know* that Nature's primary law is that of harmony and coexistence.

The media can and should show us such examples far more often than it does. When we realize that this is how Nature works, we will spontaneously examine our societies and strive to emulate that harmony among us. If our thoughts begin to shift in this direction, they will create a different atmosphere and introduce a spirit of hope and strength into our lives, even before we actually implement that spirit, since we will be aligned with Nature's life force—the Creator.

Because, as just stated, our greatest pleasure is to gain people's favor, if others approve of our actions and views we feel good about ourselves. If they disapprove of what we do or say, we feel bad about ourselves and tend to hide our actions or modify them to suit the social norm. In other words, because it is so important for us to feel good about ourselves, the media is in a unique position to shift people's actions and views.

Not surprisingly, politicians are the most ratings-dependent people in society, as their careers and very livelihood depend on their popularity. If we show them that we have changed our values, they will change theirs to follow our lead. And one of the easiest, most effective ways to tell them what we value is to show them what we want to watch on TV! If we give high ratings to shows that promote unity and camaraderie, politicians will tap into that spirit and legislate accordingly. Because politicians want to stay in office, we need to show them that, to retain their positions, they must promote what we want them to promote—unity.

When we are able to create media that promotes unity and collaboration instead of the self-glorification of celebrities, we will create an environment that *persuades* us that unity and mutual responsibility are good.

The Keys to Unity

To design a more cohesive society, whose members are responsible for one another, people need to cultivate a few ground rules.

1) Food and other necessities: First and foremost, people *must* have food security. Without the confidence that they can feed their children and themselves, people will not feel they are integral parts of society because they will constantly be fighting for food (if not physically, then mentally).

Additionally, it is imperative that people have sufficient security concerning medical services, housing, clothing, and education. All the above will vary depending on the average standard of living in each locality, but basic sustenance must be provided for all at a level that preserves their dignity as human beings and as integral members of society.

In return for guaranteeing basic sustenance, all members of society will go through some form of training, which will help them understand the interconnected and interdependent nature of our world—which is why they are receiving these services. They will learn that being in a society that ensures their well-being also entails some duties. These will relate to people's attitudes toward each other, as well as to their contribution of time or services for the common good.

For instance, making certain that all children receive basic education does not have to cost the state a penny. It can be done through unemployed teachers who voluntarily work in return for basic sustenance. This measure will contribute significantly to the social cohesion of the community, and along with the afore-mentioned training will be perceived as partaking in forming a better world, thus giving people another positive incentive to exert for the community.

2) The training: We have already mentioned the training that will help people understand the interconnected and interdependent nature of our world. The Integral Education social paradigm suggests that *every* citizen, even every *resident* of the country will partake in this training.

The training has a twofold purpose—a social one and an economic one. The economic purpose, which is more of a supplementary benefit than an actual goal in and of itself, is to furnish people with the knowledge required to support themselves in times of meager income. That part of the training will include consumer education (personal finance), so people can manage their households in an economically viable manner using limited resources.

The other, more extensive part of the course will include topics pertaining to the perception of oneself as part of a greater whole that shares a common goal. This perception is imperative to the society's cohesion. Without it, it will be each man for himself, a dog-eat-dog society.

The growing dissonance between this type of society and the aggregative direction of today's reality will no doubt heighten the already excessive pressure on people's social functioning, and the result will be society's meltdown. If that happens, as history proves and as described in the previous chapters, the Jews will be held at fault, the consequences of which are anyone's guess.

Therefore, below are topics that I believe should be included in the IE training in order to usher people into a more cohesive, and therefore sustainable worldview:

- Interconnectedness in economy, culture, and society, and what it means to each of us. This topic will detail the evolution of desires and how, at the fourth level, we wish to enjoy wealth, power, and fame, meaning self-centered pleasures, and that these desires drive us to connect, albeit negatively, in order to use one another.

- Interdependence—why we have become interdependent and how it should affect our relations on the personal, societal, and political levels. This topic should continue the explanation of the evolution of desires and show why our desires to exploit one another make us more dependent on each other. As these desires cause us to engage in ever-tightening relations, while harboring inherently ill intentions toward each other, we are growing increasingly interconnected because we want to use one another. Yet, we are equally interdependent because we are dependent on others for the satisfaction of our wants.

- Improving social, emotional, and mental capacities:
  - Learning how to cope with joblessness and the resulting financial insufficiency, stress, and depression.
  - Communication skills such as learning how to listen, how to express one's emotions and needs clearly, to respect one another, and

LIKE A BUNDLE OF REEDS

how to read body language. The goal here is to defuse aggression and establish better mutual understanding.

- o Resolving domestic conflicts in a non-violent manner.

- o Socializing as a means of learning, self-enrichment, mitigating tensions, and restoring self-esteem.

- Media consumption: As stated above, mass media is the most powerful tool in shaping our views and values. For this reason, wise consumption of media can reduce aggressive tendencies, encourage prosocial behavior, and provide essential information and understanding of the world and our place within it. To be sure, the term, "media," relates not only to the TV and radio, but also to the internet, newspapers, and some forms of pop culture, such as movies and popular music.

- Time-management skills: Learning to use one's time for personal enrichment, expansion of social circles, acquiring new or improved professional skills, and nurturing stronger and more solid family ties.

- Qualifying trainees as trainers for future courses and trainings.

Also, where physical attendance is possible, the training will be given through social activities, simulations, group work, games, and multimedia presentations. The learning will *not* be in the traditional teacher-class frontal format. Rather, the teacher and students will sit in a circle and will converse as equals, thus learning through mutual enrichment and sharing. Where physical attendance is not possible, the educational framework will be largely interactive, with examples and activities designed primarily for eLearning.

The results of such a training should be twofold: 1) understanding how to manage one's personal life in today's volatile social environment and economic instability; 2) understanding that there is a natural law galvanizing this unfolding, that that law is as stern and inexorable as gravity, and that we must therefore master these new means of coping for our own good.

While we all have to know how to manage ourselves under the Law of Interdependence, imposed on us by the Law of Bestowal, the Creator, it does not mean that everyone will have to study Kabbalah. Those who wish to study may do so, but those who have no desire to attain the Creator will contribute just as much to the "super-organism of humanity," to use the words of Christakis and Fowler, by simply living out the laws of mutual guarantee without attaining the inner workings of Creation.

Just as you do not need to be a qualified electrician to switch on the light successfully and safely, not everyone must be a Kabbalist, or an "expert in the workings of the Law of Bestowal," to use a more contemporary phrasing, to successfully and safely apply the Law of Bestowal to their lives. After all, this law exists *in order to do good* to His creations, as we have learned in Chapter 2. Therefore, all we need to learn is how to use it properly, just as we have learned how to use electricity, gravity, magnetism, and any other natural law or force to our benefit.

That said, just as electricians build the systems that everyone uses safely without any professional knowledge, Kabbalists will have to build the social and learning systems that inculcate the quality of bestowal into society, so everyone may use these systems beneficially, even without any knowledge of Kabbalah.

3) The round table: A means that is of primary importance, and hence merits an item all to itself, is the round table discussion format. In this type of discussion, all participants are of equal status and represent different, often opposing views on subjects that are critical to the well-being and soundness of the community, city, state, or country.

The goal of the deliberation is neither to reconcile differences nor to induce compromise. Rather, the goal is to find a common denominator that stands *above* the conflicts and disputes. The result of finding such an element is that the topics in dispute suddenly seem far less important than before, and pale in comparison to the unity and warmth the participants now sense toward each other. Subsequently, solutions are easily found for previously persistent conflicts in a spirit of good faith, owing to the newly discovered *common* interest.

In Israel, several organizations and movements have implemented the round table discussion format. The *Arvut* (mutual guarantee) movement, for instance, has implemented this means of deliberation *hundreds* of times, and every time this format was used, it was reported as a major success by the participants themselves. In this manner, issues that had not been resolved for years were resolved in a matter of hours.

So far in Israel, this has been tried in big cities, villages and kibbutzim, in Arab and Druz villages, bringing together the most extreme right wing Judea and Samaria settlers with Arabs from the West Bank, in the Knesset (Israeli parliament), and within struggling populations such as immigrants from Ethiopia and the former Soviet Union. These events ended with a profound sense of unity and warmth 100 percent of the time. For video-recorded testimonials and more details on the round table discussions visit http://www.arvut.org/en/round-table.

Round table discussions have been conducted around the world, as well. New York and San Francisco (USA), Toronto (Canada), Frankfurt and Nuremberg (Germany), Rome (Italy), Barcelona (Spain), St. Petersburg and Perm (Russia), are just some of many places where this form of discussion has been implemented, all enjoying the same resounding success as in Israel.

In the spirit of equality, the actual deliberations also involve the audience, and follow this procedure: A panel of individuals of diverse, often conflicting backgrounds and agendas sit around the main table. The panelists express their views on a topic declared by the host of the event.

Next, the audience asks the panelists questions, to which one or more of them replies. It is an unbreakable rule that panelists must not reproof other panelists or interfere with their words. Personal criticism is also strictly prohibited. This way, the audience hears a variety of views that do not oppose one another, but rather *complement* one another.

Subsequently, the audience divides into multiple round tables and discusses questions posed by the host in the same manner and spirit demonstrated by the panel. Finally, the tables reconvene into a general assembly and each table presents its conclusions, as well as shares its impressions from the event as a whole.

Recently, even some online round table discussions have been tried, and they, too, were very successful. Naturally, each place has its unique mentality, and each vehicle—a live event, an online meeting, or a TV broadcast—has its advantages and disadvantages. Therefore, no two events are the same. Yet, the spirit of camaraderie and the commitment to mutual guarantee that stand at the basis of every such discussion ensure the success of these unique deliberations. Although the vast majority of societies is still a long way from living out the concepts of mutual guarantee, these discussions, as the video recordings demonstrate, manage to induce a genuine sense of what living in mutual guarantee will feel like.

INTEGRALLY EDUCATED CHILDREN

While adults must assume responsibility for changing their social environments positively, the situation is much more complicated when it comes to children and youths. Here it is the responsibility of grownups—teachers and educators—whether through private initiatives or with the government's support, to build this cohesion-inducing environment.

The current education system endorses unabated competition. In and of itself, competition is natural and not inherently negative. But if we consider today's competitive culture and what it is doing to us, and even more so to our children, it is clear that we are misusing that trait.

In *No Contest: The Case Against Competition*, Alfie Kohn, a known dissident of competition, quoted psychologist, Elliot Aronson: "From the Little League ball player who bursts into tears after his team loses, to the college students in the football stadium chanting 'We're number one!'; from Lyndon Johnson, whose judgment was almost certainly distorted by his oft-stated desire not to be the first American President to lose a war, to the third grader who despises his classmate for a superior performance on an arithmetic test; we manifest a staggering cultural obsession with victory."[260]

Indeed, libraries and the internet are rife with studies indicating that competition and individualism are bad, and collaboration and cooperation are good, both at work and at school. Jeffrey Norris published a story in the News Center of UCSF, titled, "Yamanaka's Nobel Prize Highlights Value of Training and Collaboration." In that story, Norris asserted, "The lone scientist working late into the night to complete a breakthrough experiment that leads to a Eureka moment of solitary joy is a stock scene from Hollywood movies, but in reality science is a highly social endeavor."[261] Later, in the section, "Synergistic Collaboration Drives Progress," he adds, "In the open layouts of modern scientific laboratory buildings, each principal scientific investigator works with several postdoctoral fellows, graduate students and technicians, and a visitor can't tell where one lab ends and another begins. Scientific ideas and camaraderie are nurtured in the interactive environment."[262]

It is likewise at school. Numerous experiments have already been conducted on the benefits of collaboration in the education system. In an essay called, "An Educational Psychology Success Story: Social Interdependence Theory and Cooperative Learning," University of Minnesota professors David W. Johnson and Roger T. Johnson present the case for the "social interdependence" theory. In their words, "More than 1,200 research studies have been conducted in the past 11 decades on cooperative, competitive, and individualistic efforts. Findings from these studies have validated, modified, refined, and extended the theory."[263]

The authors proceed to detail what these studies had found. The researchers compared the effectiveness of cooperative learning to the commonly used individual, competitive learning. The results were unequivocal. In terms of individual accountability and personal responsibility, they concluded, "The positive interdependence that binds group members together is posited to result in feelings of responsibility for (a) completing one's share of the work and (b) facilitating the work of other group members. Furthermore, when a person's performance affects the outcomes of collaborators, the person feels responsible for the collaborators' welfare as well as for his or her own. Failing oneself is bad, but failing others as well as oneself is worse."[264] In other words, positive interdependence turns individualistic people into caring and collaborating ones, the complete opposite of the current trend of growing individualism to the point of narcissism.[265]

Johnson and Johnson distinguish between positive interdependence and negative interdependence. The positive kind entails "...a positive correlation among individuals' goal attainments; individuals perceive that they can attain their goals if and only if the other individuals with whom they are cooperatively linked attain their goals."[266] The negative one means that "individuals perceive that they can obtain their goals if and only if the other individuals with whom they are competitively linked fail to obtain their goals."[267]

In order to demonstrate the benefits of collaboration, the researchers measured the achievements of students who collaborated compared to those who competed. In their findings, "The average person cooperating was found to achieve at about two thirds of a standard deviation above the average person performing within a competitive or individualistic situation."[268]

To understand the meaning of such deviation above the average, consider that if a child is a D-average student, by cooperating, that student's grades will leap to an astonishing A+ average. Also, the Johnsons wrote, "Cooperation, when compared with competitive and individualistic efforts, tends to promote greater long-term retention, higher intrinsic motivation, and expectations for success, more creative thinking... and more positive attitudes toward the task and school."[269] In other words, not only the children benefit from this prosocial attitude, but society as a whole gains leverage.

In early 2012, I coauthored with Professor of Psychology and Gestalt-therapist, Dr. Anatoly Ulianov, a book titled, *The Psychology of the Integral Society*. The book details the essentials of IE, with specific references to today's over-competitive society. In essence, the book suggests that since competition is inherent to human nature—as detailed earlier in this book regarding the speaking degree's aspiration for wealth, power, and fame— we should not inhibit it. Instead, rather than competing to be king (or queen) of the hill, so to speak, we can foster a social atmosphere that endorses competition for the person who contributes most to others.

Specifically, those who should be declared winners are individuals who did the most to make *others* better. In a sense, it is a competition to be the one who loves others the most. Thus, children's natural drive to excel—and specifically, to excel over others—is not inhibited, allowing them to actualize their full potential while channeling it toward benefiting society instead of themselves, since the only way to win this type of competition is to be the best at being good. In this way, competition becomes a tool for initiating the quality of bestowal in children.

To foster this healthy atmosphere, peer-to-peer relations and teacher-student relations must reflect these prosocial values. This entails some modifications to the traditional teaching style. The premise in IE is that today's foremost challenge in education is not transmission of information, but rather inculcating capabilities by which to acquire information quickly and in a manner that best serves students' varying goals.

This is a shift from the traditional paradigm, which results from the fact that today's life is very different from the time of the Industrial Revolution, during which the concept of frontal lecturing of information was conceived. In the Information Age, data accumulate so quickly that past experiences can only serve as a basis for further learning. In preparation for today's adult world, schoolchildren need to learn *how* to learn more than they need to absorb information.

Additionally, because of the interconnected and interdependent nature of today's world, from early on children need to comprehend that self-interest alone will not lead to happiness. Rather, as Johnson and Johnson demonstrate, mutual consideration and openness to others will promote their chances of success and happiness more successfully.

But children need to experience the interconnectedness of the world in real life, and not just hear or talk about it. One practical way to achieve this is by transforming the classroom into a microcosm, a mini-environment, a small family where everyone cares for one another.

To that end, IE proposes that students and teachers—or "educators," as they are referred to in IE—will sit in circles, and the learning will take place through lively discussions on the subject matter. Circles place educator and students on the same level, so the educator can gently guide the discussion toward learning, and even more important, toward mutual understanding without being overbearing or domineering.

Another important issue is the school curriculum. This should reflect the interconnected nature of the world. The curriculum should also support integration of topics. Thus, fields of study such as math, physics, and biology will not be taught separately, but within the context of Nature as a whole, which is how the laws of the three disciplines actually function.

Integration should be inherent in the actual study, and it is quite likely to see students apply laws of biology to their studies in humanities. After all, humanity has already been labeled "a superorganism," so applying the laws of biology to human society seems a natural evolution.

Also notable is the point that in IE, educators are often not teachers, but *older students*. This enhances overall cohesion and camaraderie among students of different age groups, develops verbal and pedagogical skills of the young educators, and induces far deeper assimilation of information in the tutors because they have to teach it.

But most of all, when young tutors teach instead of grownup teachers, discipline issues become virtually obsolete. Because younger children naturally look up to children who are older than them by two to three years, instead of resenting the educators, as they often feel toward grownup teachers, they seek their favor and race to be the best student in the tutors' eyes. Couple that aspiration with the above-mentioned desire to be the best at being good, and you have on your hands a school atmosphere to which children will enjoy coming in the morning, and in which they will grow up to be confident and *prosocial* adults.

Befitting the purposes of IE, the learning itself will take place in groups, as it is the most advantageous form of study for nurturing social skills and for inculcating information, according to the above studies of Johnson and Johnson. Thus, a student's evaluation will not relate to his or her ability to memorize and recite in a standardized test. Rather, evaluations will be given to groups, rather than to individuals. This will enhance even further the sense of group responsibility and mutual guarantee among the students.

That said, teachers and educators will regularly send reports to parents and school administrators regarding children's social and educational progress. Because teachers will be much closer to the students than today's teaching methods allow, they will see if a problem arises with a child before it deteriorates into a major crisis.

Once a week, students should leave the school building and go on outings. To get to know the world they live in, the education system must provide them with firsthand knowledge of the institutions that affect their lives, the governing authorities, and the history and nature of the places they live in. Such outings should include museums, hikes in nearby parks, visits to agricultural communities, tours in factories, hospitals, and outings to government institutions, police stations, and so forth.

Each of these excursions will require preparation that will equip students with prior knowledge of the place they are about to visit, the role of that place in society, what it contributes, possible alternatives, and the origins of that place or institution.

For example, before an outing to the local police station, the students will research the topic of policing on the internet, if possible with specific information on the station they are about to visit. They will learn how the police came to its current mode of action, how it fits within the fabric of life in our society, and what alternatives to the police we might imagine.

In this way, children learn about the world they live in, develop creative thinking to imagine a more desirable future, practice teamwork, and improve their learning skills. Following the outing, further discussions will enable students to share what they have learned, draw conclusions, make suggestions, and compare what they have found with the notions they held regarding the topic in discussion prior to the outing.

There is much more to say about IE schools, such as regarding parents-school-student relations, approach toward homework, recommended hours at school, holidays, punishment-or-no-punishment policies, etc.. Developing this topic further is beyond the scope of this book, but the idea surrounding IE should be clear: children need to learn in an interconnected environment, and experience firsthand the benefits and fun associated with living in such an environment.

OUR PRIVILEGE, OUR DUTY, OUR TIME

One last thing needs to be mentioned regarding education of adults, youths, and children. No form of Integrated Education will succeed if it aims *only* to improve our material lives. While this is a desirable goal, it will not be achieved without a profound understanding that all of humanity is moving toward an era of interconnectedness and interdependence because *this is the Law of Nature.*

People do not need to call it "the Creator." There is no need for anyone to aspire to attain a higher, deeper, broader level of perception unless it is their will. However, people *will* have to know that equivalence of form, being like the Law of Nature, meaning interconnected, behooves us to adapt our way of life accordingly.

The ones who set the curriculum and design the study programs will have to be as just described, meaning Kabbalists. That said, Kabbalah studies will never be mandatory because only those who wish to transform themselves, to dedicate themselves to the service of others, and genuinely wish to acquire the quality of bestowal will devote themselves to this vocation.

Granted, such a social transformation is a hefty task. And yet, we Jews have been transformed before, and whether dormant or awake, the reminiscence of that transformation exists within us all. No other nation has been given the task of redeeming humanity, as have the Jews, and no other nation has been given the inherent tools to do so. It is our calling; it is our privilege; it is our duty; and it is our time.

It is out of that sense of commitment that the above suggested education method has been devised. It may sound like a rather unorthodox method, but its foundations are rooted deep within our history and deep within our souls, and its "tenets" have been tested successfully by other doctrines. It will succeed if we unite, and it will fail if we do not. As our sages said, "Great is the peace, for even when Israel idol-worship but there is peace among them, the Creator says, 'It is as though I cannot govern them because there is peace among them.'"[270]

I would like to end with a reference to the words of Baal HaSulam at the end of his "Introduction to the Book of Zohar." He concludes his introduction with a statement that if Israel should carry out their mission and bring happiness to the world through unity and acquisition of the quality of bestowal, the words of Prophet Isaiah will come true, and the nations shall join us and help us in our mission. As Baal HaSulam quotes, "Thus says the Lord God: 'Behold, I will lift up my hand to the nations, and set up my standard to the peoples: and they shall bring thy sons in their arms, and thy daughters shall be carried on their shoulders'" (Isaiah 49:22).

AFTERWORD

Humanity deserves to be united into a single family.
At that time all the quarrels and the ill will that
stem from divisions of nations and their boundaries
shall cease. However, the world requires mitigation,
whereby humanity will be perfected through each
nation's unique characteristics. This deficiency is
what the Assembly of Israel will complement.

The Rav Kook,
Orot HaRaaiah [*Lights of the Raaiah*]*, Shavuot*, p 70

It has not been easy to write this book. I have written dozens of books, but none has been as emotionally demanding or intellectually challenging. For many years now, I have known the task that stands before us, but I have always been hesitant about writing directly to my Jewish brethren. I did not wish to be perceived as condescending or overbearing, and being tediously preachy or admonitory is not high on my "To Do" list.

And yet, my Kabbalah studies with Rabash taught me that the direction in which the world is moving is en route to ending in mayhem. That is why the Rabash's father, Baal HaSulam, as well as his son, were more eager to circulate the ancient wisdom as a cure to humanity's soaring egotism than any previous Kabbalist.

Baal HaSulam was anxious about the growing global interdependence early in the 1930s, when very few people in the world were even conscious of the process. He knew that it would lead to an irresolvable crisis if humanity did not support that mutual dependence with mutual guarantee, that human nature would not be able to tolerate the contrast between interdependence and mutual aversion.

At the same time, even at that early stage in our globalization, Baal HaSulam realized that the process was irreversible, that because we are parts of a single soul, a single desire, we are inherently connected. He also knew, as did all the sages quoted in this book, that the goal for which we were created was not for people to be strangers and hateful, but to bond and unite through the quality of bestowal.

Today we see how right he was. We are hopelessly ill-connected, and vehemently resentful of it. Our social systems, such as economy, health, and education, assume that ill will is the foundation of human relations, and therefore each entity shores itself up through regulations, legislations, and solicitors.

But this *modus operandi* is unsustainable. As good families assume goodwill among family members, all members of humankind must learn to trust one another.

However, as shown throughout the book, because our egos constantly evolve and emphasize our uniqueness rather than our unity, we need a method to help us achieve unity atop our disparity, without suppressing or nullifying it. That method is rooted in the spiritual patrimony of our people, and is the gift of the Jews to humanity, the salvation that the nations all await from the Jews.

The gift can be handed down through the wisdom of Kabbalah, through Integral Education, by the means that Baal HaSulam suggested in *The Nation*, or by any other means that will yield a fundamental change in human nature from divisiveness to unity, from animosity to empathy and care. If we achieve that unity, then the more we differ in our character, the stronger and warmer will be our bond. As Rabbi Nathan Sternhertz described it, "It primarily depends on man, who is the heart of Creation, and on whom everything depends. This is why 'Love your neighbor as yourself' is the great *klal* ["rule," but also "collective"] of the Torah, to include in unity and peace, which is the heart of the vitality, persistence, and correction of the whole of Creation, by people of differing views being included together in love, unity, and peace."[271]

Indeed, the beauty of our people is in its unity, its cohesion. Our nation began as a group of individuals who shared a common desire: to discover life's essential force. We discovered that it was, in a word, "love," and we discovered it because we developed that quality within us. That force of love united us, and in the spirit of love, we sought to share our discovery with anyone who willed it.

Over time, we have lost our connection, first with each other, then with the force we discovered through our bond. But now the world needs us to rekindle that bond, first among us, and subsequently among the whole of humanity.

We are a gifted nation, a nation with the gift of love, which is the quality of the Creator. Receiving this gift is the goal for which humanity was created, and we are the only conduit by which this love can flow to all the nations. Since the dawn of humanity, "never have so few owed so much to so many," to paraphrase Winston Churchill's words. And yet, never have so few been capable of giving so much to so many.

Indeed, as Baal HaSulam says, "It is upon the Israeli nation to qualify itself and all the people of the world ... to develop until they take upon themselves that sublime work of the love of others, which is the ladder to the purpose of Creation, which is *Dvekut* [equivalence of form] with Him."[272]

NOTES

---

1 Rav Yehuda Leib HaLevi Ashlag (Baal HaSulam), *The Writings of Baal HaSulam*, "The Writings of the Last Generation" (Ashlag Research Institute: Israel, 2009), 813-814.

2 *Masechet Derech Eretz Zuta*, Chapter 9.

3 *Masechet Yoma*, p 9b.

4 Rabbi Kalonymus Kalman Halevi Epstein, *Maor va Shemesh* (*Light and Sun*), Parashat (Portion) Balak

5 Jean M. Twenge and W. Keith Campbell, *The Narcissism Epidemic: Living in the Age of Entitlement* (New York: Free Press, A Division of Simon & Schuster, Inc. 2009), 1.

6 Jean M. Twenge and W. Keith Campbell, *The Narcissism Epidemic*, 1-2.

7 Rav Moshe Ben Maimon (Maimonides), *Mishneh Torah* (*Repetition of the Torah*, a.k.a. *Yad HaChazakah* (*The Mighty Hand*)), Part 1, "The Book of Science," Chapter 1, Item 3.

8 Rabbi Yehuda HaLevi, *The Kozari*, "First Essay," item 31, 60.

9 HaRav Avraham Yitzchak HaCohen Kook, *Letters of the RAAIAH* 3 (Mosad HaRav Kook, Jerusalem, 1950), 194-195.

10 Yehuda Leib Arie Altar (ADMOR of Gur), *Sefat Emet* [*Truthful Lips*], Parashat Yitro [Portion, Jethro], TARLAZ (1876).

11 Rabbi Shmuel Bornstein, *Shem MiShmuel* [*A Name Out of Samuel*], Haazinu [Give Ear], TARAP (1920).

12 ibid.

13 Rav Yehuda Leib HaLevi Ashlag (Baal HaSulam), *The Writings of Baal HaSulam*, "Peace in the World," 464-5.

14 Rav Yehuda Leib HaLevi Ashlag (Baal HaSulam), *The Writings of Baal HaSulam*, "The Love of God and the Love of Man," 486.

15 Yehuda Leib Arie Altar (ADMOR of Gur), *Sefat Emet* [*Truthful Lips*], Parashat Yitro [Portion, Jethro], TARLAZ (1876).

16 *Sefer HaYashar* [*The Book of the Upright One*], Portion Noah, Parasha 13, item 3.

17 *Pirkey de Rabbi Eliezer* [*Chapters of Rabbi Eliezer*], Chapter 24

18 ibid.

19 Rav Moshe Ben Maimon (Maimonides), *Mishneh Torah* (*Yad HaChazakah* (*The Mighty Hand*)), Part 1, "The Book of Science," Chapter 1, Item 1.

20 Maimonides, *Yad HaChazakah* (*The Mighty Hand*), Part 1, "The Book of Science," Chapter 1, Item 3.

21 Rav Yehuda Leib HaLevi Ashlag (Baal HaSulam), *The Writings of Baal HaSulam*, "Peace in the World," 406-7.

22 Maimonides, *Yad HaChazakah* (*The Mighty Hand*), Part 1, "The Book of Science," Chapter 1, Item 3.

23 *Midrash Rabbah, Beresheet*, Portion 38, Item 13.

24 ibid.

25 Maimonides, *Yad HaChazakah* (*The Mighty Hand*), Part 1, "The Book of Science," Chapter 1, Item 3.

26 ibid.

27 ibid.

28 Rabbi Meir Ben Gabai, *Avodat HaKodesh* [*The Holy Work*], Part 3, Chapter 27.

29 Elimelech of Lizhensk, *Noam Elimelech* (*The Pleasantness of Elimelech*), *Likutei Shoshana* ("Collections of the Rose") (First published in Levov, Ukraine, 1788), URL: http://www.daat.ac.il/daat/vl/tohen.asp?id=173.

30 Shlomo Ephraim Luntschitz, *Keli Yakar* [*Precious Vessel*] , Concerning Beresheet [Genesis], 32:29.

31 Chaim ibn Attar, in *Ohr HaChaim* [*Light of Life*], Bamidbar [Numbers], Chapter 23, Item 8, https://sites.google.com/site/magartoratemet/tanach/orhahaym.

32 Baruch Shalom Ashlag (Rabash), *The Writings of Rabash*, Vol. 1, Article no. 9, 1988-89 (Israel: Ashlag Research Institute, 2008), 50, 82, 163.

33 Rabbi Meir Ben Gabai, *Avodat HaKodesh* [*The Holy Work*], Part 2, Chapter 16.

34 Rabbi Isaiah HaLevi Horowitz (The Holy Shlah), *Toldot Adam* [*The Generations of Man*], "The House of David," 7.

35 Rav Yehuda Ashlag (Baal HaSulam), *The Writings of Baal HaSulam*, "Introduction to the Preface to the Wisdom of Kabbalah," 155.

36 Rav Yehuda Ashlag (Baal HaSulam), *The Writings of Baal HaSulam*, "Introduction to the Book of Zohar," 432.

37 Rabbi Shlomo Ben Yitzhak (RASHI), *The RASHI Interpretation on the Torah*, "Concerning Exodus," 19:2.

38 *Midrash Tanah De Bei Eliyahu Rabah*, Chapter 28.

39 *Midrash Tanhuma, Nitzavim*, Chapter 1.

40 Ithak Eliyahu Landau, Rabbi Shmuel Landau, *Masechet Derech Eretz Zutah*, Chapter 9, items 28-29 (Vilna: Printer: Rabbi Hillel, 1872), 57-58.

41 Babylonian Talmud, *Masechet Berachot* [Treaties Blessings] p 44a; Maimonides, *Mishneh Torah*, "Rules of Blessings," Chapter 8, Rule 14; Rav Moshe Cordovero (the Ramak), *An Orchard of Pomegranates*, Gate 23, Chapter 5; and numerous others.

42 Rabbi Isaiah HaLevi Horowitz (The Holy Shlah), *Masechet Pesachim*, Sixth Interpretation, (27); Rabbi Menachem Nachum of Chernobyl, *Maor Eynaim* [*Bright Eyes*], *Lech Lecha* [Go Forth], Rabbi Tzadok HaCohen of Lublin, *The Thoughts of the Diligent*, item 19, and many others.

43 Yehuda Ashlag, *Talmud Eser HaSephirot* [*The Study of the Ten Sephirot*], Part 1, *Histaklut Pnimit* (Inner Reflection), Chapter 2, items 10-11 (Jerusalem: M. Klar, 1956), 17.

44 ibid.

45 Rabbi Isaiah HaLevi Horowitz (The Holy Shlah), *Masechet Pesachim*, Sixth Interpretation, (27).

46 Rabbi Nathan Sternhertz, *Likutey Halachot* [*Assorted Rules*], "Rules of Teflat Arvit [Evening Prayer]," Rule no. 4.

47 Yehuda Ashlag, *Talmud Eser HaSephirot* [*The Study of the Ten Sephirot*], Part 1, "Introduction to the Study of the Ten Sephirot," items 104-105 (Jerusalem: M. Klar, 1956), 31.

48 Rav Yehuda Leib HaLevi Ashlag (Baal HaSulam), *The Writings of Baal HaSulam*, "Introduction to the Book, Panim Meirot uMasbirot [Shining and Welcoming Face]" (Ashlag Research Institute, Israel, 2009), 150.

49 Rabbi Itzhak Luria (the Holy ARI), *Tree of Life*, Gate 39, Article no. 3.

50 Rabbi Meïr Leibush ben Iehiel Michel Weiser (The MALBIM), *Concerning 1 Kings, 8:10*, Section, "Explanation of the Matter."

51 Rabbi Pinhas HaLevi Horovitz, *Sefer HaMikneh* [*The Deed Of Purchase*], *Masechet Kidhushin* [Treatise Betrothal], p 82a.

52 Rabbi Abraham Ben David, (The RABaD), *The RABaD Commentary on The Book of Creation*, Chapter 2, Study no. 2.

53 Rav Yehuda Leib HaLevi Ashlag (Baal HaSulam), *The Writings of Baal HaSulam*, "The Freedom," 415.

54 Rabbi Nathan Neta Shapiro, *Reveals Deep Things, Parashat Shemot* [Exodus].

55 Rav Yehuda Leib HaLevi Ashlag (Baal HaSulam), *The Writings of Baal HaSulam*, "Introduction to the Book, Panim Meirot uMasbirot [Shining and Welcoming Face]," 134.

56 Maimonides, *Yad HaChazakah* (*The Mighty Hand*), Part 1, "The Book of Science," Chapter 1, Item 1.

57 Rav Yehuda Leib HaLevi Ashlag (Baal HaSulam), *The Writings of Baal HaSulam*, "Introduction to The Book of Zohar," items 43-44, 444.

58 Rav Baruch Shalom Ashlag (the Rabash), *The Writings of Rabash*, "On My Bed at Night" (Ashlag Research Institute, Israel, 2008), 129.

59 Rabbi Shimon Bar Yochai (Rashbi), *The Book of Zohar* (with the *Sulam* [Ladder] Commentary by Baal HaSulam, New Zohar, *Parashat Toldot*, vol. 19, item 31 (Jerusalem), 8-9.

60 Rabbi Isaiah HaLevi Horowitz (The Holy Shlah), *Masechet Sukkah* [Treatise, *Sukkah*], Chapter, "Torah, Light" (13).

61 Rabbi Naphtali Tzvi Yehuda Berlin (The NATZIV of Volojin), *Haamek Davar* [*Delve Deep in the Matter*] about Beresheet [Genesis], Chapter 47:28.

62 *Pirkey de Rabbi Eliezer* [Chapters of Rabbi Eliezer], Chapter 24.

63 Rav Yehuda Leib HaLevi Ashlag (Baal HaSulam), *The Writings of Baal HaSulam*, "Introduction to the Book, Panim Meirot uMasbirot [Shining and Welcoming Face]," 134.

64 Rabbi Isaiah HaLevi Horowitz (The Holy Shlah), *In Ten Utterances*, "Sixth Utterance."

65 Rabbi Shimon Ashkenazi, *Yalkut Shimoni* [*The Shimoni Anthology*], Micah, Chapter 7, continuation of intimation no. 556.

66 *Midrash Rabah*, *Shemot* [Exodus], Portion 30, Paragraph 17.

67 Ramchal (Rav Moshe Chaim Lozzatto), *Daat Tevunot*, 154, 165.

68 Rav Yehuda Leib HaLevi Ashlag (Baal HaSulam), *The Writings of Baal HaSulam, Shamati* [I Heard], Article no. 5, "Lishma Is an Awakening from Above, and Why Do We Need an Awakening from Below," 518.

69 *Midrash Rabah, Kohelet* [Ecclesiastes], Portion 1, Paragraph 34.

70 Rabbi Isaiah HaLevi Horowitz (The Holy Shlah), "Gate of Letters," Item 60, "Satisfaction."

71 Ramchal (Rav Moshe Chaim Lozzatto), *Daat Tevunot*, 154, 165.

72 Maimonides, *Yad HaChazakah* (*The Mighty Hand*), Part 1, "The Book of Science," Chapter 1, Item 3.

73 Rabbi Shlomo Ben Yitzhak (RASHI), *The RASHI Interpretation on the Torah*, "Concerning Exodus, 19:2."

74 Babylonian Talmud, *Masechet Sanhedrin*, p 94b.

75 "It is called 'The Land of Canaan' because all who wish to dwell in it must be subjugated by suffering all his days" (Rav Chaim Vital (Rachu), *The Book of Knowledge of Good, Bo* [Come]).

76 *Midrash Tehilim* [Psalms], Psalm no. 34.

77 Rabbi Chaim Thirer, *A Well of Living Waters, Toldot* [Generations], Chapter 25 (contd.).

78 Rabbi Behayei Ben Asher Even Halua, *Rabeinu Behayei, Concerning Beresheet* [Genesis], 46:27.

79 Rabbi Yisrael Segal, *Netzah Yisrael* [*The Might of Israel*], Chapter 5.

80 Rabbi Abraham Ben Meir Ibn Ezra, *Ibn Ezra, Concerning the Song of Songs*, 7:3.

81 Rabbi Menahem Nahum of Chernobyl, *Maor Eynaim* [*Light of the Eyes*], *Beresheet* [Genesis].

82 Jonathan ben Natan Netah Eibshitz, *Yaarot Devash* [*Honeycombs*], Part 1, Treatise no. 13 (contd.).

83 Abraham Ben Mordechai Azulai, Introduction to the book, *Ohr Ha-Chama* (*Light of the Sun*), 81.

84 Rav Chaim Vital, *The Writings of the Ari, Tree of Life*, Part One, "Rav Chaim Vital's Introduction," 11-12

85 The Vilna Gaon (GRA), *Even Shlemah* [*A Perfect and Just Weight*], Chapter 11, Item 3.

86 Rav Yitzhak Yehuda Yehiel of Komarno, *Notzer Hesed* [*Keeping Mercy*], Chapter 4, Teaching 20.

87 Rav Yitzhak HaCohen Kook (the Raiah), *Orot* [*Lights*], 95.

88 Rav Yitzhak HaCohen Kook (the Raiah), *Otzrot HaRaiah* [*Treasures of the Raiah*], 2, 317.

89 Rav Moshe Chaim Lozzatto (Ramchal), *Adir BaMarom* [*The Mighty One On High*], "Explanation of Daniel's Dream" (Warsaw, 1885).

90 Rav Moshe Chaim Lozzatto (Ramchal), *The Commentary of Ramchal on the Torah, BaMidbar* [Numbers].

91 Rav Yitzhak HaCohen Kook (the Raiah), *Letters the Raiah* vol. 2, 34.

92 Rav Yitzhak HaCohen Kook (the Raiah), *Orot* [*Lights*], 16.

93 Rav Yehuda Leib HaLevi Ashlag (Baal HaSulam), *The Writings of Baal HaSulam*, "Messiah's Shofar," 457.

94 Rav Yehuda Leib HaLevi Ashlag (Baal HaSulam), *The Writings of Baal HaSulam*, "The *Arvut* [Mutual Guarantee]," item 28, 397.

95 Ramchal, *The Commentary of Ramchal on the Torah, BaMidbar* [Numbers].

96 Yitzhak Isaac Hever Wildman, *Beit Olamim* [*A House Everlasting*] (Warsaw, 1889), 130a.

97 Rav Moshe Chaim Lozzatto (Ramchal), *Essay of the Tenets*, (Oybervisha (Felsövisó) Romania, 1928), 15. URL: http://www.hebrewbooks.org/33059.

98 Rav Abraham Isaac HaCohen Kook (Raaiah) (appeared in *HaPeles*, a rabbinical magazine, Berlin, Germany, 1901) (A. The Vocation of Israel and Its Nationality, Chapter 1, p 26).

99 HaRav Avraham Yitzchak HaCohen Kook, *Letters of the RAAIAH* 3, 194-195.

100 Rav Abraham Isaac HaCohen Kook (Raaiah), *Ein Ayah* [*A Hawk's Eye*], Shabbat 1, p 188.

101 Rabbi Naphtali Tzvi Yehuda Berlin (The NATZIV of Volojin), *Haamek Davar* [*Delve Deep in the Matter*], Concerning *Devarim* [Deuteronomy], Chapter 27:5.

102 Johannes Reuchlin, *De Arte Cabbalistica* (Hagenau, Germany: Tomas Anshelm, March, 1517), 126.

103 A Book of Jewish Thoughts, ed. J. H. Hertz (London: Oxford University Press, 1920), 134.

104 Paul Johnson, A History of the Jews (New York: First Perennial Library, 1988), 585-6.

105 Thomas Cahill, The Gifts of the Jews: How a Tribe of Desert Nomads Changed the Way Everyone Thinks and Feels (New York: Nan A. Talese/ Anchor Books (imprints of Doubleday), 1998), 3.

106 Rabbi Shmuel Bornstein, Shem MiShmuel [A Name Out of Samuel], Miketz [At the End], TARPA (1921).

107 Rav Yehuda Leib HaLevi Ashlag (Baal HaSulam), The Writings of Baal HaSulam, "The Wisdom of Kabbalah and Philosophy," 38.

108 Terrot Reavely (T.R.) Glover, The Ancient World (US: Penguin Books, 1944), 184-191.

109 Herman Rauschning, The Beast From the Abyss (UK: W. Heinemann, 1941), 155-56.

110 Josephus Flavius, The Wars of the Jews, Chapter 1, translated by William Whiston in The Works of Flavius Josephus (UK: Armstrong and Plaskitt AND Plaskitt & Co., 1835), 564.

111 William Whiston, The Works of Flavius Josephus, 565.

112 Yaakov (Jacob) Leschzinsky, The Jewish Dispersion (Israel, World Zionist Organization, 1961), 9.

113 The Holy ARI, Eight Gates, Shaar HaPsukim [Gate to Verses], Parashat Shemot [Portion, Exodus].

114 Rabbi Naphtali Tzvi Yehuda Berlin (The NATZIV of Volojin), Haamek Davar [Delve Deep in the Matter] about Devarim [Deuteronomy], Chapter 27:5.

115 Rav Yehuda Ashlag (Baal HaSulam), The Writings of Baal HaSulam, "Essays of Shamati [I Heard]," essay no. 86, "And They Built Store-Cities," 591.

116 ibid.

117 Rav Yehuda Ashlag (Baal HaSulam), The Writings of Baal HaSulam, "The Arvut [Mutual Guarantee]," 393.

118 Rav Yehuda Ashlag (Baal HaSulam), The Writings of Baal HaSulam, "A Handmaid that Is Heir to Her Mistress," 454.

119 Midrash Rabah, "Song of Songs," Parasha no. 4, 2nd paragraph.'

120 Babylonian Talmud, *Masechet Pesachim*, p 87b.

121 Yehuda Leib Arie Altar (ADMOR of Gur), *Sefat Emet [Truthful Lips]*, *Parashat Yitro* [Portion, Jethro], TARLAZ (1876).

122 Hillel Tzaitlin, The Book of a Few (Jerusalem, 1979), 5.

123 Rav Yehuda Ashlag (Baal HaSulam), *The Writings of Baal HaSulam*, "The Love of God and the Love of Man," 486.

124 Johann Wolfgang von Goethe, *Wilhelm Meisters Lehrjahre* (Berlin (Germany), Johann Friedrich Unger, 1795-1796), 359.

125 Glover, *The Ancient World*, 184-191.

126 Ernest van den Haag, *The Jewish Mystique* (US, Stein & Day, 1977), 13.

127 *Blaise Pascal*, Pensees, trans. W.F. Trotter, Introduction by T.S. Eliot (Benediction Books, 2011), 205.

128 Ashlag, *Talmud Eser HaSephirot* (*The Study of the Ten Sephirot*), Part 1, "Introduction to the Study of the Ten Sephirot," 31.

129 Babylonian Talmud, *Masechet Hulin*, p 89a.

130 Maimonides, *The Writings of Rambam* [Maimonides], "The Ethics of the Rambam to His Son, Rabbi Abraham."

131 Elimelech of Lizhensk, *Noam Elimelech* (*The Pleasantness of Elimelech*), *Parashat Beshalach* [Portion, "When Pharaoh Sent"].

132 Rabbi Jacob Joseph Katz, *Toldot Yaakov Yosef* [*The Generations of Jacob Joseph*], *BeShalach* [When Pharaoh Sent], item 1.

133 Rabbi Katz, *Toldot Yaakov Yosef* [*The Generations of Jacob Joseph*], *Acharei* [After the Death], item 1.

134 Jonathan ben Natan Netah Eibshitz, *Yaarot Devash* [*Honeycombs*], Part 2, Treatise no. 10.

135 Rav Yehuda Ashlag, *Shamati* [*I Heard*], essay no. 144, "There Is a Certain People" (Canada, Laitman Kabbalah Publishers, 2009), 300.

136 ibid.

137 Rav Avraham Kook (Raaiah), *Essays of the Raaiah*, vol. 1, pp 268-269.

138 Rav Yehuda Ashlag (Baal HaSulam), *The Writings of Baal HaSulam*, "The Freedom," 420.

139 Babylonian Talmud, *Masechet Sanhedrin*, 97b.

140 Babylonian Talmud, *Masechet Avodah Zarah* [Idolatry], 2b.

141 New Testament, John 4:22.

142 New Testament, Romans 3:1-2

143 Martin Gilbert, *Churchill and the Jews* (UK, Simon & Schuster, 2007), 38.

144 *A Book of Jewish Thoughts*, ed. J. H. Hertz (Oxford University Press, 1920), 131.

145 Professor Huston Smith, *The Religions of Man* (New York: Harper-Collins, 1989).

146 Leo Tolstoy, "What is the Jew?" quoted in *The Final Resolution*, p 189, printed in Jewish World periodical, 1908.

147 Paul Johnson, *A History of the Jews* (New York, First Perennial Library, 1988), 2.

148 Rav Yitzhak HaCohen Kook (the Raiah), *Essays of the Raaiah*, vol. 2, "The Great Call for the Land of Israel," 323.

149 Aaron Soresky, "The ADMOR, Rabbi Yehuda Leib Ashlag ZATZU-KAL—Baal HaSulam: 30th Anniversary of His Departure," *Hamodia*, 9, Tishrey, TASHMAV (September 24, 1985).

150 Rav Avraham Kook (Raaiah), *Essays of the Raaiah*, vol. 1, pp 268-269.

151 Rav Yehuda Ashlag (Baal HaSulam), *The Writings of Baal HaSulam*, "The Writings of the Last Generation," 853.

152 Rav Yehuda Ashlag (Baal HaSulam), *The Writings of Baal HaSulam*, "The Writings of the Last Generation," 841.

153 Henry Ford, *The International Jew—The World's Foremost Problem* (The Noontide Press: Books On-Line), 40.

154 Henry Ford, *The International Jew—The World's Foremost Problem* (The Noontide Press: Books On-Line), 8.

155 Henry Ford, *The International Jew—The World's Foremost Problem* (The Noontide Press: Books On-Line), 28.

156 John Adams, in a letter to F. A. Vanderkemp (16 February 1809), as quoted in *The Roots of American Order* (1974) by Russel Kirk.

157 Mark Twain, *The Complete Essays of Mark Twain*, "Concerning The Jews" (published in Harper's Magazine, 1899), Doubleday, [1963], pg. 249.

158 Martin Gilbert, *Churchill and the Jews* (UK, Simon & Schuster, 2007), 16.

159 Ronnie S. Landau, *The Nazi Holocaust: Its History and Meaning* (US: Ivan R. Dee, 1994), 137.

160 "Decisions Taken at the Evian Conference On Jewish Refugees" (July 14, 1938), Jewish Virtual Library, url: http://www.jewishvirtuallibrary.org/jsource/Holocaust/evian.html.

161 Yad Vashem, *Shoah Resource Center*, "Evian Conference," url: http://www1.yadvashem.org/odot_pdf/Microsoft%20Word%20-%206305.pdf.

162 Yad Vashem, "Related Resources, Evian conference," url: http://www1.yadvashem.org/yv/en/exhibitions/this_month/resources/evian_conference.asp.

163 Baal HaSulam, *The Writings of Baal HaSulam*, "The Writings of the Last Generation," 832-833.

164 Eric Hoffer, *Los Angeles Times*, May 26, 1968.

165 From M.L. King Jr., "Letter to an Anti-Zionist Friend," Saturday Review XLVII (August 1967), p. 76 Reprinted in M.L. King Jr., "This I Believe: Selections from the Writings of Dr. Martin Luther King Jr."), url: http://www.internationalwallofprayer.org/A-022-Martin-Luther-King-Zionism.html.

166 U.S. Department of State, "Report on Global Anti-Semitism (January 5, 2005), url: http://www.state.gov/j/drl/rls/40258.htm.

167 Ruth Ellen Gruber, "Anti-Semitism without Jews," url: http://www.annefrank.org/ImageVaultFiles/id_11774/cf_21/Gruber.pdf.

168 Robert Fulford, "Anti-Semitism without Jews in Malaysia," *National Post* (October 6, 2012), url: http://fullcomment.nationalpost.com/2012/10/06/robert-fulford-anti-semitism-without-jews-in-malaysia/.

169 ibid.

170 Rabbi Nathan Neta Shapiro, *Reveals Deep Things, Parashat Shemot* [Exodus].

171 *The Haftarah* (parting) reading follows the Torah reading on each Sabbath and on Jewish festivals and fast days. The reader of the haftarah is called maftir.

172 "Diaspora," *The Jewish Encyclopedia*, url: http://www.jewishencyclopedia.com/articles/5169-diaspora.

173 ibid.

174 ibid.

175 Dan Cohn-Sherbok, *The Paradox of Anti-Semitism* (UK: Continuum International Publishing Group, 2006), XIV (Preface).

176 William Whiston, *The Works of Flavius Josephus*, 565.

177 ibid.

178 Josephus Flavius, *Antiquities of the Jews*, XIV, 115.

179 "Diaspora," *The Jewish Encyclopedia*, url: http://www.jewishencyclopedia.com/articles/5169-diaspora.

180 Norman Roth, *Jews, Visigoths, and Muslims in Medieval Spain: cooperation and conflict* (The Netherlands, E.J. Brill, 1994), 2.

181 ibid.

182 Jane S. Gerber, *The Jews of Spain: A History of the Sephardic Experience* (New York, Free Press; November 2, 1992), Kindle edition.

183 ibid.

184 Rabbi Shimon Bar Yochai (Rashbi), *The Book of Zohar* (with the Sulam [Ladder] Commentary by Baal HaSulam, Noah, vol. 3, item 385 (Jerusalem), 132.

185 Michael Grant, *From Alexander to Cleopatra: the Hellenistic World* (New York: Charles Scribner & Sons, 1982), 75.

186 Quoted in *The Treasury of Religious and Spiritual Quotations* (US: Readers Digest, January 1, 1994), 280.

187 Jacob Rader Marcus, *The Jew in the Medieval World: A Sourcebook: 315-1791*, (US: Hebrew Union College Press, 1999), 60-61.

188 ibid.

189 Dr. Erwin W Lutzer with Steve Miller, *The Cross in the Shadow of the Crescent: An Informed Response to Islam's War with Christianity* (Harvest House Publishers, Oregon, 2013), 65.

190 Israel Zinberg, *History of Jewish Literature: The Jewish Center of Culture in the Ottoman Empire*, Vol 5 (New York, Ktav Pub. House, 1974), 17.

191 Hillel Tzaitlin, *The Book of a Few* (Jerusalem, 1979), 5.

192 Sol Scharfstein, *Understanding Jewish History: From Renaissance to the 21st Century* (Printed in Hong Kong, Ktav Publishing House, 1997), 163-164.

193 Salo W. Baron, *The Menorah Treasury: Harvest of Half a Century*, "Ghetto and Emancipation: Shall We Revise the Traditional Views?" (Philadelphia: Jewish Publication Society of America, 1964), 52.

194 Salo W. Baron, *The Menorah Treasury: Harvest of Half a Century*, "Ghetto and Emancipation: Shall We Revise the Traditional Views?", 54-55.

195 Rabbi Shmuel Bornstein, *Shem MiShmuel [A Name Out of Samuel]*, *VaYakhel* [And Moses Assembled], TAR'AV (1916).

196 *Assimilation and Community: The Jews in Nineteenth-Century Europe*, Ed: Jonathan Frankel, Steven J. Zipperstein (UK, Cambridge University Press, 1992), 8.

197 *Assimilation and Community: The Jews in Nineteenth-Century Europe*, Ed: J. Frankel, S.J. Zipperstein, 12.

198 "Emancipation," *Jewish Virtual Library*, url: http://www.jewishvirtuallibrary.org/jsource/judaica/ejud_0002_0006_0_05916.html.

199 Werner Eugen Mosse, *Revolution and Evolution: 1848 in German-Jewish History* (Germany, J.C.B. Mohr (Paul Siebeck) Tubingen, 1981), 255-256.

200 Eugen Mosse, *Revolution and Evolution: 1848 in German-Jewish History*, 260.

201 Donald L. Niewyk, *The Jews in Weimar Germany* (New Jersey, Transactions Publishers, New Brunswick, 2001), 95.

202 Niewyk, *The Jews in Weimar Germany*, 84.

203 ibid.

204 Cohn-Sherbok, *The Paradox of Anti-Semitism*, XIV (Preface).

205 Adolf Hitler, *Mein Kampf* (US: Noontide Press, 2003), 51.

206 Ludwig Feuerbach, *The Essence of Christianity*, trans. Marian Evans (London: John Chapman, 1843), 113.

207 *Assimilation and Community: The Jews in Nineteenth-Century Europe*, Ed: Jonathan Frankel, Steven J. Zipperstein, 12.

208 "Conservative Judaism," *The Encyclopaedia Britannica*, url: http://www.britannica.com/EBchecked/topic/133461/Conservative-Judaism.

209 Michael A. Meyer, *Response to Modernity: A History of the Reform Movement in Judaism* (Detroit, US: Wayne State University Press, 1995), 226.

210 Meyer, *Response to Modernity: A History of the Reform Movement in Judaism*, 227.

211 *Reform Judaism: A Centenary Perspective*, Adopted in San Francisco – 1976 (Oct. 27, 2004), url: http://ccarnet.org/rabbis-speak/platforms/reform-judaism-centenary-perspective/.

212 ibid.

213 Rav Yehuda Ashlag (Baal HaSulam), *The Writings of Baal HaSulam*, "Introduction to the Book of Zohar," 450-453.

214 ibid.

215 ibid.

216 ibid.

217 Rav Yehuda Ashlag (Baal HaSulam), *The Writings of Baal HaSulam*, "The Nation," 489.

218 ibid.

219 Rav Yehuda Ashlag, *Shamati [I Heard]*, essay no. 144, "There Is a Certain People" (Canada, Laitman Kabbalah Publishers, 2009), 300.

220 Adolf Hitler, *Mein Kampf* (The Noontide Press: Books On-Line), 219, url: www.angelfire.com/folk/bigbaldbob88/MeinKampf.pdf.

221 "Roger Federer: 2016 Games possible," *Associated Press*, July 26, 2012, url: http://espn.go.com/olympics/summer/2012/tennis/story/_/id/8202865/roger-federer-leaning-competing-rio-2016-body-holds-up.

222 "School for Culture Education, Be'eri Program," *Shalom Hartman Institute*, June 26, 2011. url: http://medaon.org/files/zehutariel.pdf.

223 *Pirkey de-Rabbi Eliezer (Chapters of Rabbi Eliezer)*, Chapter 24.

224 *Midrash Rabah, Beresheet* [Genesis], *Parasha* 39, Paragraph no. 3.

225 Rabbi Behayei Ben Asher Iben Haluah, *Rabeinu* [our Rav] *Behayei, Beresheet* [Genesis] 15:6.

226 *Associated Press*, "Recession will likely be longest in postwar era," MSNBC (March, 2009), http://www.msnbc.msn.com/id/29582828/wid/1/page/2/.

227 Clive Thompson, "Are Your Friends Making You Fat?", *The New York Times* (September 10, 2009), http://www.nytimes.com/2009/09/13/magazine/13contagion-t.html?_r=1&th&emc=th.

228 ibid.

229 ibid.

230 ibid.

231 "Nicholas Christakis: The hidden influence of social networks" (a televised talk, quote taken from minute 17:11), TED 2010, http://www.ted.com/talks/nicholas_christakis_the_hidden_influence_of_social_networks.html.

232 Anthony Giddens, *Runaway World: How Globalization Is Reshaping Our Lives* (N.Y., Routledge, 2003), 6-7.

233 Dr. Leandro Herrero, *Homo Imitans: The Art of Social Infection: Viral Change in Action* (UK: Meetingminds Publishing, 2011), 4.

234 ibid.

235 Pascal Lamy "Lamy underlines need for 'unity in our global diversity,'" World Trade Organization (WTO) (June 14, 2011), http://www.wto.org/english/news_e/sppl_e/sppl194_e.htm.

236 Christian Jarrett, Ph.D, "Mirror Neurons: The Most Hyped Concept in Neuroscience?" *Psychology Today* (December 10, 2012), url: http://www.psychologytoday.com/blog/brain-myths/201212/mirror-neurons-the-most-hyped-concept-in-neuroscience.

237 ibid.

238 Nicholas A. Christakis, James H. Fowler, *Connected: The Surprising Power of Our Social Networks and How They Shape Our Lives -- How Your Friends' Friends' Friends Affect Everything You Feel, Think, and Do* (USA, Little, Brown and Company, January 12, 2011), 305.

239 Maimonides, *Yad HaChazakah* [*The Mighty Hand*], Part 1, "The Book of Science," Chapter 1, Item 3.

240 Rav Yehuda Ashlag (Baal HaSulam), *The Writings of Baal HaSulam*, "The Freedom" (Israel: Ashlag Research Institute, 2009), 414.

241 "Evolution Can Occur in Less Than Ten Years," *Science Daily* (June 15, 2009), http://www.sciencedaily.com/releases/2009/06/090610185526.htm.

242 John Cloud, "Why Your DNA Isn't Your Destiny," *Time Magazine* (January 06, 2010), url: http://www.time.com/time/magazine/article/0,9171,1952313,00.html.

243 ibid.

244 Rav Yehuda Ashlag (Baal HaSulam), *The Writings of Baal HaSulam,* "The Freedom," 419.

245 ibid.

246 ibid.

247 Rav Yehuda Ashlag (Baal HaSulam), *The Writings of Baal HaSulam,* "The Freedom," 419.

248 ibid.

249 Quoted from the film, *Crossroads: Labor Pains of a New Worldview,* by Joseph Ohayon, published December 31, 2012, on Youtube, url: https://www.youtube.com/watch?v=5n1p9P5ee3c, 2:53 from the beginning.

250 Thomas J. Murray, Ed.D., "What is the Integral in Integral Education? From Progressive Pedagogy to Integral Pedagogy," *Integral Review* (June 2009), Vol. 5, No. 1, p 96.

251 http://en.wikipedia.org/wiki/Integral_education.

252 http://www.merriam-webster.com/dictionary/homeostasis.

253 T. Irene Sanders and Judith McCabe, PhD, *The Use of Complexity Science: a Survey of Federal Departments and Agencies, Private Foundations, Universities, and Independent Education and Research Centers,* October 2003, Washington Center for Complexity & Public Policy, Washington, DC. url: www.hcs.ucla.edu/DoEreport.pdf.

254 Rav Yehuda Ashlag (Baal HaSulam), *The Writings of Baal HaSulam,* 44.

255 Jon R Katzenbach & Douglas K Smith, *The Wisdom of Teams: Creating the High-Performance Organization* (US: Harvard Business School Press, January 1, 1992), 37-38.

256 *U.S. Department of Education,* "Media Guide—Helping Your Child Through Early Adolescence," http://www2.ed.gov/parents/academic/help/adolescence/index.html.

257 *University of Michigan Health System,* "Television and Children," http://www.med.umich.edu/yourchild/topics/tv.htm.

258 ibid.

259 Barbara M. Newman and Philip R. Newman, *Development Through Life: A Psychosocial Approach* (Belmont, CA: Wadsworth Cengage Learning, 2008), 250.

260 Elliot Aronson, *The Social Animal*, pp 153-54, quoted in: Alfie Kohn, *No Contest: The Case Against Competition* (NY: Houghton Mifflin Company, 1986), 2.

261 Jeffrey Norris, "Yamanaka's Nobel Prize Highlights Value of Training and Collaboration," *UCSF News Section* (October 11, 2012), url: http://www.ucsf.edu/news/2012/10/12949/yamanakas-nobel-prize-highlights-value-training-and-collaboration.

262 ibid.

263 David W. Johnson and Roger T. Johnson, "An Educational Psychology Success Story: Social Interdependence Theory and Cooperative Learning," *Educational Researcher* 38 (2009): 365, doi: 10.3102/0013189X09339057.

264 Johnson and Johnson, "Educational Psychology Success Story," 368.

265 Books on narcissism in the American society abound. Good examples are: Jean M. Twenge and W. Keith Campbell, *The Narcissism Epidemic: Living in the Age of Entitlement* (New York: Free Press, A Division of Simon & Schuster, Inc. 2009), and Christopher Lasch, *The Culture of Narcissism: American Life in an Age of Diminishing Expectations* (USA: Norton & Company, May 17, 1991).

266 ibid.

267 ibid.

268 Johnson and Johnson, "Educational Psychology Success Story," 371.

269 ibid.

270 *Midrash Rabah, Beresheet* (Genesis), Portion 38, Paragraph 6.

271 Rabbi Nathan Sternhertz, *Likutey Halachot [Assorted Rules]*, "Rules of Tefilat Arvit [Evening Prayer]," Rule no. 4.

272 Rav Yehuda Ashlag (Baal HaSulam), *The Writings of Baal HaSulam*, "The *Arvut* [Mutual Guarantee]," item 28 (Ashlag Research Institute, Israel, 2009), 393.

The Author
and
His Work

Professor of Ontology and Theory of Knowledge, a PhD in Philosophy and Kabbalah, and an MS in Medical Cybernetics, Michael Laitman is dedicated to promoting positive changes in educational policies and practices through innovative ideas and solutions to the most pressing social, cultural, and educational problems of our time. He has introduced a new approach to education, incorporating modes of thinking that derive from our interdependent and interconnected reality.

In his meetings with Mrs. Irina Bokova, Director General of UNESCO, and with Dr. Asha-Rose Migiro, Deputy Secretary-General of the UN, he discussed current global challenges and his vision for their solution. In recent years, he has worked closely with many international institutions and has participated as a keynote speaker in several international events in Tokyo (with the Goi Peace Foundation), Arosa (Switzerland), and Düsseldorf (Germany), and with the International Forum of Cultures in Monterrey (Mexico). These events were organized with the support of UNESCO.

Dr. Michael Laitman has been featured in the following publications, among others: *Corriere della Sera*, the *Chicago Tribune*, the *Miami Herald*, *The Jerusalem Post*, and *The Globe* and on RAI TV and Bloomberg TV.

Dr. Laitman has spent his entire life exploring human nature and society, seeking answers to the meaning to life in our modern world. The combination of his academic background and extensive knowledge make him a sought-after world thinker and speaker. Dr. Laitman has written over 40 books that have been translated into 18 languages, all with the goal of helping individuals achieve harmony among them and with the environment around them.

NOTABLE PUBLICATIONS

Self-Interest vs. Altruism in the Global Era:
How society can turn self-interests into mutual benefit

Self-Interest vs. Altruism in the Global Era presents a new perspective on the world's challenges, regarding them as necessary consequences of humanity's growing egotism, rather than a series of errors. In that spirit, the book suggests ways to *use* our egos for society's benefit, rather than trying to suppress them.

...Stating that society's future relies on cooperation
of people to work together for society, stating that
much of society's degradation in recent decades has

been the result of narcissism and greed, *Self Interest vs. Altruism* is a curious and recommended read.

James A. Cox, Editor-in-Chief, Midwest Book Review

The Psychology of the Integral Society

The book presents a series of dialogs between Professors Michael Laitman and Anatoly Ulianov. Together, they shed light on the principles of an eye-opening approach to education. Absence of competition, child rearing through the social environment, peer equality, rewarding the givers, and a dynamic makeup of group and instructors are only some of the new concepts introduced in this book. *The Psychology of the Integral Society* is a must-have for all who wish to become better parents, better teachers, and better persons in the integrated reality of the 21st century.

"What's expressed in The Psychology of the Integral Society should get people thinking about other possibilities. In solving any difficult problem, all perspectives need to be explored. We spend so much time competing and trying to get a leg up that the concept of simply working together sounds groundbreaking in itself."

Peter Croatto, *ForeWord Magazine*

A Guide to the New World: Why mutual guarantee is the key to our recovery from the global crisis

Why does 1% of the world population own 40% of the wealth? Why are education systems throughout the world producing unhappy, poorly educated children? Why is there hunger? Why are food prices rising when there is more than enough food for everyone? Why are there still countries where human dignity and social justice are nonexistent? And when and how will these wrongs be made right?

These questions touch the hearts of all of us. The cry for social justice has become a demand around which all can unite. We all long for a society where we can feel safe, trust our neighbors, and guarantee the future of our children. In such a society, all will care for all, and mutual guarantee—where all are guarantors of each other's well-being—will thrive.

Despite all the challenges, change is possible, and we can find a way to implement it. Therefore, *A Guide to the New World* is a positive, optimistic book, which helps us pave the way toward that goal.

Connected—by Nature's Law

Our society is not as it was a few years ago. We have grown apart, become "hooked" on technological innovations, and many of our social ties amount to online "friendships." It seems that mutual concern and kindness to strangers have disappeared. Unfortunately, without them we have no society, and so they *must* return. The only question is "How to make it happen?"

Connected—by Nature's Law is an innovative book on social awareness. Presenting a comprehensive picture of reality and the process that humanity is undergoing, the book offers tools for using the major personal and social shifts we're going through to our benefit.

The book suggests a "healthcare program for humanity" by solidifying the ties between us on all levels—family, community, national, and international. The sooner we implement the program, the sooner we will find ourselves enjoying tranquil, happy, and *meaningful* lives.

The Book of Zohar:
Annotations to the Ashlag commentary

The Book of Zohar is an age-old source of wisdom and the basis for all Kabbalistic literature. Since its appearance, it has been the primary, and often only source used by Kabbalists.

Written in a unique and metaphorical language, *The Book of Zohar* enriches our understanding of reality and widens our worldview. Rav Yehuda Ashlag's unique *Sulam* (Ladder) commentary allows us to grasp the hidden meanings of the text and "climb" toward the lucid perceptions and insights that the book holds for those who study it.

Contact Information

For Inquiries and information
contact@bundleofreeds.com
www.bundleofreeds.com

USA

2009 85th St., Suite 51
Brooklyn NY, USA -11214
Tel. +1-917-6284343

CANADA

1057 Steeles Avenue West
Suite 532
Toronto, ON – M2R 3X1 Canada
Tel. +1 416 274 7287